Going Home to the Fifties

Going Home
to the

FIFTIES

by *Bill Yenne*

Last Gasp
San Francisco

Published by Last Gasp of San Francisco

© 2002 O.G. Publishing Corp.

Distributed by Last Gasp of San Francisco
777 Florida Street
San Francisco, CA 94110
www.lastgasp.com
email: gasp@lastgasp.com

Produced by the AGS BookWorks division
of American Graphic Systems, Inc.
PO Box 460313
San Francisco, CA 94146
www.agsbookworks.com

Text and design © 2002 Bill Yenne

ISBN 0-86719-564-9
Printed and bound in China

Designed by Bill Yenne with design assistance from Azia Yenne.
Proofreading by Joan B. Hayes. Captioning by Bill Yenne, with thanks to
Special Resource Study Route 66, United States Department of the
Interior, National Park Service, NPS D-4.

All illustrations were provided by the
Alvarado Collection, with the following exceptions:

David Bolzano Images: 26-27
The Dwight D. Eisenhower Library: 23
The M.J. McPike Collection
 (© American Graphic Systems, Inc.): 89, 90
Sierra Solana Library, Advertising Archives:
 1-3, 6, 7, 10 (bottom), 11, 15, 18 (bottom), 22, 24,
 33-36, 38-44, 47, 49, 50, 52-57, 59-64, 66-69, 72-
 73, 76-77, 80, 84 (top), 91, 92, 94, 96-98, 100-107,
 109-111, 114-115, 117, 118 (bottom), 120 (top),
 121-123, 124 (bottom), 125-127, 128 (bottom),
 129-130, 133, 134 (bottom), 136 (bottom), 137,
 138 (bottom), 139, 141
Western Museum of Ethnography: 125 (top),
 128 (top), 131-132, 134 (top), 136 (top), 139 (top)

Table of Contents

Going Home

This book is a celebration of American home life in the fifties, arguably the happiest and most contented era in American history. America in the fifties was a time and place that was unique in the history of the world. The economic power and prosperity of the United States, as compared to the rest of the world, was immense. The adults who lived during that era believed that they had worked hard to achieve that prosperity. The young people who grew up amid the prosperity had never known different. For them, it was the way it was, the way it should be.

While most of the developed world had emerged from World War II drained, damaged and exhausted, the United States emerged as a robust economy that far overshadowed that of any other nation. Undamaged by warfare, the United States had greatly expanded its industrial capacity and had invested greatly in new technology.

Despite the Damocles sword represented by the

6

RIGHT: A MERCURY WAGON, 1952.

OPPOSITE: BODY BY FISHER, 1950.

With record high prosperity and record low unemployment, Americans became consumers. After the privation and shortages of nearly two decades of depression and war, Americans went on a shopping spree. As they bought new homes and new cars, the economy boomed. More Americans bought new kitchen appliances and new living room furniture than at any time before — and probably since.

And never before had there been such an enormous gulf between the "look" of the new and that of the "old" that was being replaced. Consumer goods had not been available on a large scale since before the 1940s, and relatively few were available or sold in the depressed 1930s.

The new houses, cars, appliances and furniture of the fifties had a radical new styling that was as far as it could be from the old styles that

recently released nuclear genie and the festering inequities that would be addressed by the civil rights movement of the sixties, the fifties were — and are remembered as — the best years of the twentieth century for most middle-class Americans from coast to coast.

Girls yearn for this romantic Love-Gift

THE GIFT THAT STARTS THE HOME

Give her the
real Valentine
Love-Gift

No. 2221

No. 2217

Thrill your sweetheart with a Lane Hope Chest—dearest way in the world to say "I love only you." Even more—it's a precious sanctuary for trousseau treasures—the real love-gift that starts the home!

The only Tested Aroma-Tight Chest in the world with Lane's exclusive patented features. Backed by free moth insurance policy written by one of the world's largest insurance companies. The Lane Company, Inc., Dept. L, Altavista, Virginia. In Canada: Knechtels, Ltd., Hanover, Ontario.

Chest No. 2210 $49.95   Slightly higher in the West and Canada

No. 2221 (at top). 18th Century drawer design in Honduras Mahogany. A beautiful addition to any bedroom, living room, dining room or hallway. Hand-rubbed satin finish.

No. 2217 (in center). A modern design in matched Mahogany finished in a soft wheat color. Hand-rubbed, polished finish. Equipped with Lane's patented automatic tray.

No. 2210 (at bottom). Front center panel of V-matched New Guinea Wood, bordered with cross-grained Zebra Wood, diamond matched American Walnut. Top of V-matched American Walnut. Has Lane's patented automatic tray. Hand-rubbed and polished finish.

LANE *Cedar Hope Chest*

9

dated back to the 1920s or before. The fifties were stylistically unique — on purpose. Along with style, the new consumer goods of the fifties brought consumers vast new technology. Most homes now had washers and dryers for the first time, and innovations such as dishwashers became common. Most of all, television sets completely altered the American home in the fifties. Television became a universal medium that brought a nation together and created, for the first time in United States history, a national culture that we take for granted today.

The economic, technological and cultural changes that occurred in the United States after World War II were abrupt and widespread. They set the course that we still follow to this day, but they represent the admittedly naive era when the postwar American culture was new and fresh, and the future was still perceived as being brighter than the present.

10

ABOVE: STUDENTS IN AN AMERICAN CLASSROOM, 1951. TOP: AN ARGUS C-20 KIT WITH FLASH BULBS. OPPOSITE: HOME MOVIES RECORD THE GOOD LIFE.

Make your vacation live a lifetime...
with a
lifetime
Bell & Howell !

Just as clear, bright and colorful as you *saw* it . . . just as lively and real as you *lived* it . . . that's the way Bell & Howell movies will make your memories live forever!

Nearly half a century's experience in meeting Hollywood's exacting demands has given Bell & Howell the *extra* skill and precision that must go into a camera to give you steady, *life-like* pictures on your screen.

Every Bell & Howell camera has these extra qualities built in for life. They'll make your memories live a lifetime!

$139.95

172-B. This 8mm camera takes crisp, clear life-like and steady pictures in color or black-and-white . . . true Bell & Howell movies! Features instant magazine loading, world's finest lens, exclusive B&H positive viewfinder (you see *exactly* what you get), five easy-to-set camera speeds, accurate footage indicator, easy-to-read exposure guide. And like all Bell & Howell products, it is guaranteed for life.*

*During the life of the product any defect in workmanship or material will be remedied free (except transportation).

Price subject to change without notice.

*You buy for life
when you buy*

Bell & Howell

11

For adults who had experienced two decades of war and depression, the fifties were the end of the rainbow. For the vast baby boom generation, who grew up during the decade, it was all they had ever known. Peace and prosperity were a welcome reality rather than merely a cliche. The two cars in the suburban garage, the mother at home baking cookies for the kids and the family nights around the new television represented a lifestyle of quiet comfort for millions of Americans.

By the end of the sixties, the style and culture of the fifties would be an object of rebellion for the baby boomers, but as that generation begins to reach middle age and to reflect on their lives and experiences, the fifties are now an object of nostalgia and warm, happy memories. It's time to recapture those memories, or to experience all of those wonderful days from the fabulous fifties for the very first time.

It's time to go home to the fifties. ✳

ABOVE: DRESSED FOR TREE-TRIMMING IN THE PROSPEROUS YEARS. OPPOSITE: BICYCLES, LEMONADE AND CONTESTS.

What Were the Fifties?

The fifties were a magical time when everything seemed to work, and to work well. Most adult Americans lived in larger and more modern homes than their parents. Most children lived in two-parent families and attended public schools that were safe and orderly. In most families, dad went to work at a job that paid better than any job he'd ever had and his paycheck easily covered the family's expenses with enough left over for a little savings

RIGHT: SANTA CLAUS AS UNCLE SAM.

toward a vacation and education for the kids. Indeed, most children in the United States could look forward to college, a dream that was far more attainable than at any time in the previous decades. While dad went off to work and the kids went off to school, mom typically stayed home to do the housework, but she usually had more and better appliances than her mother had ever dreamed of. Washing machines, clothes dryers and dishwashers, all of which had

OPPOSITE: WHAT LIFE WAS REALLY ABOUT.

14

been a relative rarity in homes before the fifties, became almost essential equipment by the end of the decade.

The fifties were a wonderful decade by their stark contrast to the decades that came before, and they seem so naively blissful in retrospect only when we forget that they were preceded by the thirties and forties. The fifties were a unique crossroads of prosperity and advancing technology that provided a life and lifestyle in the United States that could hardly have been imagined before World War II, and which seems almost too good to be real today.

During the fifties, home ownership increased dramatically, and in those homes, the marriage rate for people in their twenties and thirties was at its highest level ever and the divorce rate declined. Meanwhile, the birth rate climbed sharply, creating the much-discussed baby boom and a building boom of schools that led to what would later be described as the golden age of public education.

The magical moments of the past often take on a mythical

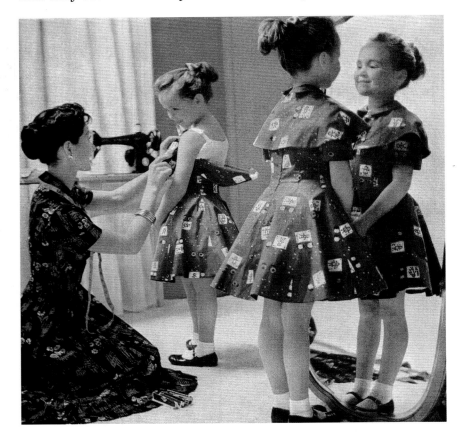

LEFT: THE TWINS IN THEIR FIRST SCHOOL DRESSES.

is for Mother

Housewife, cook, chauffeur, hostess, teacher, glamor girl—she does dozens of jobs well. And make no mistake! She works just as hard as her grandma but gets much more done. Why? Because things like wash-and-wear fabrics and stain-resistant paints are making home routine jobs easier all the time. Who's responsible for so many of these new time-saving products? Mother's little helper—oil.

dimension that makes them seem larger than life and more vivid than reality. Their stylized form frequently seems more real than the reality of what actually happened. Such is the case with the fifties. When fifties culture was "revived" in the seventies through such vehicles as the musical *Grease*, it was a version of reality in which certain elements of the culture were exaggerated for effect. In the fifties, most teenage girls did not wear poodle skirts, at least not most of the time. Nor did large numbers of teenage boys wear black leather jackets.

Today we tend to think of the fifties in terms of such cultural milestones as the birth of rock & roll and the advent of the beat generation, but at the time, these were mere anomalies. The beats and the rockers would influence the culture of future generations far more than they would influence the life and culture of the fifties. People such as Elvis Presley and Jack Kerouac are icons of the fifties as the fifties are remembered today, but they were not icons of contemporary culture

17

ABOVE: THOUGHTS ABOUT MOTHER, CIRCA 1956. OPPOSITE TOP: MOM AND SIS IN A STARRING ROLE.

formed by artists such as Doris Day, Connie Francis or Perry Como. The fifties were a time that was very much characterized by a lack of exaggeration and an abhorrence for non-conformity.

in the fifties. During the fifties, teenagers owned Elvis Presley records and college students read Kerouac, but the music on the radio in most American homes was more than likely being per-

More than radio, however, television would become the dominant communications medium in most American homes in the fifties. Virtually unknown in American homes in the forties, television would become the center of family life by the early fifties.

The essential cultural ethos of the fifties was that it was a time of plenty. In the sixties, the baby boomers, the children of the fifties, would revolt against the "materialism" of the fifties, which they perceived as being shallow and one-dimensional. However, that which their parents had embraced was seen

LEFT AND ABOVE: NEW FRIENDS, FIRST DAY OF SCHOOL.

ABOVE: MOM TAKES THE TODDLERS TO THE MATINEE, CIRCA 1950.

as a deserved reward rather than shallow "materialism" for its own sake. As noted in the preceding section, the parents of the baby boomers had endured wartime rationing in the forties, when staples from sugar to gasoline were severely rationed. They could, as the baby boomers could not, also remember the Great Depression of the thirties, when many people could not afford new shoes, much less a new car.

The fifties were a time of plenty. They were an era when virtually everybody could afford the shoes they needed, when most families could afford a new car and many families could afford two cars. More important, they were a time when dad didn't have to roam the country looking for seasonal work as his father or uncle might have during the thirties. Revisionists have complained

20

ABOVE: TWO WEEK'S WORTH OF CARGO FOR THIS 1959 FORD COUNTRY SQUIRE STATION WAGON.

not have the careers that their daughters would value in the eighties or nineties, but they did have more leisure than their mothers had had — or her daughters would have.

The fifties dawned as a time when dreams of a better life had finally come true. Wages were up, the economy expanded and technology gave consumers a profusion of products that could not have been imagined a just a dozen years earlier.

that mom stayed home to do the housework, but forget that in the previous generation, moms were forced to take in washing to keep bread on the family table. Most of the "fifties moms" did

The fifties were a time when dreams came true. The fifties were a magical and wonderful time. The fifties were, for most people, the decade at the end of the rainbow. ❊ ❊

21

THE PHOTOGRAPH SHOWS EVERY PERSON, ITEM AND SPANIEL THAT TRAVELLED IN THE WAGON FROM *SATURDAY* TO *SATURDAY*.

When Were the Fifties?

One might begin this tale with the phrase: "Long ago and far away there was a magical, wonderful place and time. . ." The fifties were magical and they were wonderful, but they were also very real. So *when* did the fifties actually occur? Did the fifties begin on January 1, 1950 and end at midnight on December 31, 1959? Or did they coincide with the presidency of Dwight Eisenhower and last from January 1953 to January 1961? Today we often think of the fifties more as a cultural milieu or even as a state of mind than as a time in history, so to answer this question, we should really ask ourselves when the "fifties" cultural milieu really existed in the United States.

The prosperity that made the fifties possible began after World War II, but not immediately after. The war ended in September 1945, but many of the millions of American soldiers that had gone overseas would not be reunit-

RIGHT: LOOKING INTO THE NEW HOUSE THROUGH A THERMOPANE WINDOW.

OPPOSITE: THE EISENHOWER INAUGURAL PARADE, JANUARY 1953.

ed with their families until at least 1946. American industry, which had tooled up to produce an unprecedented volume of radios, vehicles, uniforms and medical supplies for the war effort, would not fully retool for consumer goods until 1947 or 1948. In Detroit, the major carmakers quickly rushed out their first civilian automobiles since the handful of 1942 models that had appeared in the fall of 1941, but the styling of the 1946 models was almost invariably just a variation on the 1942 styling. It would not be until the 1949 and 1950 model years that there would be the radical changes in styling that we think of in terms of the look of fifties cars.

Technologically, the forties ended and the fifties began in about 1950 or 1951. Automotive styling was one thing, but so too were the availability of large appliances that changed the look of the American home. Television, which separated fifties culture from all that had gone before, was a mere novelty as late as 1948, but in 1951, the Federal Communications Commission allocated new VHF frequency bands that permitted a sudden proliferation of new stations, and the number of American homes with a television set

ABOVE: A DREAM DATE IN A 1957 PONTIAC CUSTOM CATALINA.

shot from nine percent to almost seventy percent by 1955, and to almost ninety percent by 1959.

Historically, the fifties are recalled as an era when nothing memorable happened. This is not literally true, of course, but by comparison it comes close. Even the most absent-minded history student remembers that the forties were consumed by World War II and the beginning of the Cold War, and that the sixties were marked by the such milestone events as the Kennedy and King assassinations, the first Apollo moon landings, the civil rights struggle and the beginning of the Vietnam War. By comparison, the fifties had few historical turning points for Americans. Even the brutal Korean War, which took place during the fifties, is often referred to as "the forgotten war."

For Americans, politically, the fifties were the Eisenhower era. Dwight David "Ike" Eisenhower was a well-respected — if not beloved — war hero, who is best remembered for his immense managerial and planning skills rather than battlefield exploits. He assembled and managed the greatest coalition armed force in human

25

❋

history and defeated Nazi Germany. In 1952, he was elected president with a comfortable 55 percent of the vote. In 1956, he was reelected with 57 percent. During the eight years that spanned the most prosperous years of the twentieth century, Eisenhower served two presidential terms virtually unblemished by the distractions of scandal, war, economic recession, civil strife or assassination that have punctuated the histories of nearly all subsequent presidencies. Eisenhower was the perfect father figure for the fifties. His public image was that of an honest and honorable man. Nobody thought to question his ethicacy or his credibility. Maybe it was the times and maybe it was the man.

Thanks to some degree to Eisenhower's fatherly, but detached leadership style, the fifties were a time of conservative optimism. People appreciated what they had and assumed that tomorrow was as bright as today. However, times do change and conservative optimism evolved into a complacency that bred a desire for change. Yet it was that optimism that would lead a new generation to think of new frontiers.

The end of the Eisenhower administration was the end of an era. When the fifties father figure handed the reins of leadership to the energetic, young John F. Kennedy on January 20, 1961, the sixties had definitely begun. The quiet, comfortable years had given way to an era of activism and dynamism. ❉ ❉

TOP: *A CONFIDENT YOUNG BRIDE'S FIRST DINNER PARTY. A NEW LIFE IN A DECADE OF PROMISE.* OPPOSITE: *FAMILY FUN.*

New Fun for Everyone!

Paint your own 5-piece Lith-o-Ware® DECORATOR TRAY KITS

Wonderful for family fun, personal pleasure...prized gifts...or profitable hobby!

Everyone can always use more trays—for snacks, TV parties, picnics, barbecues . . . and as decorative pieces. You'll be extra proud of trays you paint yourself.

Here's How Easily It's Done

The tray design you select to paint is pre-drawn, right on the tray. No color mixing required—you simply fill in numbered sections, and in no time you've painted your trays with all the colorful artistry Lith-O-Ware's designers put into them. *Just like having the artist guide your hand.*

No other paint-it-yourself kit gives you so much for your money. That's why you'll want one kit for yourself . . . and more to give to family and friends. You'll find Lith-O-Ware Decorator Tray Kits in leading department and variety stores . . . toy, gift and hobby shops.

No. 510 Maypole Design

Here's What You Get in Your Lith-O-Ware Kit

- One 17-1/2" x 12-3/4" Hostess Tray, pre-drawn, ready to paint (your choice of 4 designs)
- Four pre-drawn matching 6-1/2" x 4-1/2" Snack Servers plus one *extra* practice tray.
- Eight genuine Sap-O-lin colors . . . acid-alcohol-resistant, non-toxic . . . approved by PARENTS' magazine.
- Two professional artists' brushes, two paint cups.
- A full-color reproduction of your selected design.
- An easy-to-follow instruction book.

  Use your kit box as an easel and for storage . . . no mess . . . no muss!

Lith-O-Ware Products, Inc., 4610 W. 21st St., Chicago 50, Ill.   Canadian Distributor: Johnson Rose Co., Montreal

Choose your design from the four shown
(One shown in kit box)

No. 530 Still Life Design   No. 520 Abstract Design   No. 540 Floral Design

A priceless value at only **$4 95** West Coast Slightly Higher

4-Piece Lith-O-Ware Decorator Plate Sets

$2 95 West Coast Slightly Higher

After you've painted the four antique motor cars on these 10-in. metal plates by the simple, easy Lith-O-Ware fill-in method, you'll have a set of *beautiful* porcelain-like pieces that are truly collector's items. Set includes four pre-drawn plates, Sap-O-lin paint, brushes—plus four Easy-Stick fasteners, and "How to Paint" Book.

No. 610 Service Plate Set

29

AMERICAN TOYS

AMERICAN-MADE TOYS FOR

These American-made toys are on sale at your local stores...

Two-Way Electronic
WALKIE-TALKIES

This Electronic Walkie Talkie actually operates over long distances, electro-magnetically. Each unit is regular telephone size with dial controls to operate movable antenna. Has wave-length channel selector and secret-message compartment. Thrilling toy can be used as room-to-room or house-to-garage telephone. Ages 5 to 15. $3.95.

REMCO INDUSTRIES, INC.
113 No. 13th Street
Newark, N. J.

Junior Size
POOL TABLE

A handsome, authentic pool table that will make any 8 to 15 year old the envy of the neighborhood! Table is 28" high, measures 44½" by 25". Rail and legs are ivory-colored with contrasting maroon corners, diamonds and leg tips. Green, cloth-covered playing surface. With set of balls, 2 cues, triangle, instruction book. $29.95.

THE BURROWES CORPORATION
200 Fifth Avenue
New York 10, N. Y.

37 Piece
METALTONE
ENSEMBLE
DINNERWARE

Perfect for playing "party." Gaily colored, moulded plastic cake plates, cups, saucers, tea service, goblets, sherbets, flatware, candelabras (with make-believe candles) and napkin holder...all finished in Banner's Metaltone (silverlike) finish. For every 4 to 12 year old hostess. $5.98.

BANNER PLASTICS CORPORATION
200 Fifth Avenue, N. Y. 10, N. Y.

"Buttons and Bows"
SEWING SET

Everything a pint-size seamstress will love! A sweet, squeezable "drink-wet" doll, 12" high, with voice and sleeping eyes. Ready-made dress and bonnet, plus other outfits all cut out and ready to sew. Laces, buttons, ribbons, sewing equipment, instruction book, too. All in smart carrying case. Wonderful for ages 4 to 9. $7.98.

THE SUN RUBBER COMPANY
Barberton, Ohio

Playtime's #304
FOLDING
DOLL STROLLER

When a dolly's old enough to sit up by itself, it goes out with "mommy" in a stroller, of course! This faithful replica of a real stroller fits a 26" doll; folds up for storage. Shopping bag attached to the gay plaid body; frame is baked aluminum enamel. Even a foot rest—and rubber tires! For ages 2 to 6. $4.25

PLAYTIME PRODUCTS, INC.
Warsaw, Indiana

Revell's "Young Plumber"
PLAY SET

Ideal educational, action toy. Includes large plumber's truck with built-in water tank, lift-up hood revealing motor. Wheels can be removed with aid of jack and wrench. Complete set of plumber's tools, assorted pipes, fittings, bath tub, vise, etc. Made of super-tough Dow 475 Styron. Ages 4 to 8. $1.98.

REVELL, INC.
Venice, California

A Treasure House of Fun!
TOY FUN BOOK

Keeps youngsters fascinated by the hour, even on rainy days, indoors! Everything about toys is here: pages of toys to color, toys and games to make, cut-outs and puzzles. Delightful stories, too! 128 large pages, as in other Seahorse Fun Books. For boys and girls of grade school age. Sturdy, quality paper, stiff paper covers. $1.00.

THE SEAHORSE PRESS, INC.
Pelham 65, N. Y.

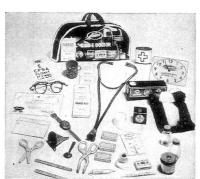

AMSCO
KIDD-E-DOCTOR

Everthing a little boy needs to play "Doctor"...and, for the little girl, there's a wonderful "Kidd-E-Nurse" kit, too. Each plastic satchel contains: realistic play instruments and accessories, even genuine sterilized Johnson and Johnson First Aid Products. $1.98.†

AMERICAN METALS
SPECIALTIES CORP.
Hatboro, Pa.

*trademark †prices slightly higher in West and South   *trademark †prices slightly higher in West and South   *trademark †prices slightly higher in West and South   *trademark †prices slightly higher in West and South

AMERICAN GIRLS AND BOYS

... or write manufacturer for name of nearest dealer.

AMERICAN TOYS

Complete Coloring Set
SENIOR ARTS PAINT BOX

Develop children's natural artistic talents with this large, attractive paint box, completely equipped. A varied assortment of top quality art materials. Set includes three types of paint...brush, mixing pan, colored crayons and outline pictures. Ages 6 to 15. $4.00. Other sets from $1.00 to $3.00.

MILTON BRADLEY CO.
Springfield 2, Mass.

White Christmas
SPARKL-TEX*

A delightful, non-flammable decoration for your Christmas Tree...mantle...and every home holiday decoration. Glittering aluminum flakes in silver or silver-red-green combination give sparkling frost-crystal effect when sprinkled over fireproofed cotton "snow." 32" x 64" strip, packed in cellophane bag. 98c.

UNION WADDING COMPANY
Pawtucket, R. I.

A Cinch To Play! MAGNUS
STUDENT ACCORDION

Here's a real instrument that keeps all standards of the modern piano-accordion. Full, vibrant tone covers more than 1½ octaves. Beautifully constructed in rich, lightweight plastic with 20 treble buttons, 4 bass. Easy song instructions included. Number (not note) system has 6 to 12 year olds playing without lessons! $12.95.

MAGNUS HARMONICA CORP.
439-451 Freylinghuysen Ave.
Newark 5, New Jersey

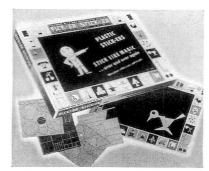

Absorbing, Educational
PICK-ER STICK-ER*

A creative toy that keeps little fingers busy...but clean! The magic of molecules makes Pick-er Stick-er's gaily colored Vinylite shapes stick to the highly polished board over and over again. No scissors. No paints. No paste. Your 2 to 8 year olds will delight in creating new designs by the hour. $1.50.†

THE ATLANTIC PLASTICS CO.
Cleveland 6, Ohio

"STURDEE"
The Sturdy Steed

As lovable and cuddly as a real pony, this life-like plush horse is a wonderful aid in teaching toddlers to walk. Its durable steel frame will safely support *any* child, and Dad too. Sturdy, generous hand-grip assures a safe, steerable ride. In handsome Russet Brown or Jet Black chew-safe colors. $9.98 to $14.98.

METH TOY COMPANY, INC.
33-35 East 21st Street
New York 10, N. Y.

Playtime's #308
FOLDING DOLL COACH

For every proud "mommy" age 3 to 9—to take dolly out for a daily airing. It's a carbon copy of a real baby's coach—big enough for a 22" doll. Folds up for easy storage. Has maroon vinyl-leatherette body, white trim; visor-hood to shade the sun; foot brake; rubber tires; sturdy baked aluminum enamel frame. $8.00.

PLAYTIME PRODUCTS, INC.
Warsaw, Indiana

Structo
BOTTOM DUMP

Your young builder will love this real-life replica of a construction dump-truck. Everything about it—from the realistic diesel motor to the extra-large, heavy duty rubber wheels—says "action"! Universal coupler connects Bottom-Dump body to tractor...turn of crank opens bottom door for dumping. For 2 to 9 year olds. $5.95.†

STRUCTO MANUFACTURING CO.
Route 75
Freeport, Illinois

So Real!
"BABEE-BEE" DOLL

Her arms and legs move like a real baby's! She cries, she sleeps, she wets — and little girls, age 2 to 6, adore her! BABEE-BEE wears matching diaper, knitted booties, and gay little coat to keep her warm. Has her own nursing bottle, too. 13" long, made of squeezable, huggable rubber (can't break) with Vinyl plastic head. $3.98.

THE SUN RUBBER COMPANY
Barberton, Ohio

31

*trademark †prices slightly higher in West and South   *trademark †prices slightly higher in West and South   *trademark †prices slightly higher in West and South   *trademark †prices slightly higher in West and South

Home To The Suburbs

From the late forties through the mid-fifties, housing patterns in the United States changed dramatically, and this changed American culture. During that period, more people moved to new single-family homes than at any previous time in American history.

At the end of World War II, 80 percent of Americans lived in rented apartments in cities. During the fifties, over half of these people

32

would move into their own homes. Since the housing in most cities consisted of high-density apartment buildings, most of those seeking single-family homes left the cities for towns and villages on the fringes of urban areas. They were neither urban nor rural, but they were attached to urban areas, so they were known as *sub*urban areas, or suburbs. Before World War II, the areas known as suburbs were often

RIGHT: A TRIP TO THE STORE.

OPPOSITE: GRANDMA ARRIVES!

working class neighborhoods that had grown up around factories on the periphery of cities. However, after the war, the term had a completely different meaning, and it was applied to residential areas that were evolving on the distant fringes of urban areas. Many of these new residential suburbs were previously rural areas, or they had been sparsely populated middle class or white-collar commuter suburbs before the war. By the early fifties, the population density here was suddenly and rapidly increasing, changing the nature of both the suburbs and the cities around which they now blossomed.

The postwar suburbs, at least initially, offered and afforded the attractive ambiance of a quiet, bucolic lifestyle, with broad lawns and safe streets instead of

34

❋

TOP: BUNDLED UP SNUGLY FOR THE TRIP TO SCHOOL.

ABOVE: A FAMILY DRIVE, VISITING THE NEIGHBORS IN THE NEW 1959 EDSEL.

crowded, bustling city centers. Such a change had always been attractive, but it had also been out of reach for most people for reasons of economics and mobility. People moved to the suburbs in droves during the late forties and the fifties because the postwar economy had made them more prosperous and more mobile.

Of course, the majority of the white-collar jobs that would be held by the people moving to the suburbs would still be in urban areas, so a new noun was added to the American lexicon. As the suburban-dwelling workers commuted to their urban jobs, they became *commuters*. The idea of commuting was made more attractive by

ABOVE: BAUHAUS AT THE SCHOOLHOUSE: A PIET MONDRIAN-INSPIRED FACADE BY OWENS-ILLINOIS FOR A TYPICAL SUBURBAN GRADE SCHOOL, 1958.

dramatic improvements in roads and highways, and by an equally dramatic rise in car ownership. Twice as many people owned cars in 1950 as in 1935, and by the late fifties, the numbers of registered automobiles and licensed drivers had reached parity for the first time. Prosperity and mobility made the suburbs possible and helped to create the celebrated fifties lifestyle.

Villages that had previously been a comfortable distance from the cities were turned into suburbs, but this process did not satisfy the demand for suburbs. As is axiomatic in the context of the American entreprenureal spirit, when something doesn't exist, an entrepreneur will create it.

The concept of the housing development (an entire neighborhood or small town built at one time by a single developer) had occurred before, such as in the boom years of the twenties, but never on a scale as would be seen in the decade after the end of World War II.

Because the traditional central cities had been fully developed and had little open space left for large-scale housing projects, most of the new communities were created in previously rural

37

❋

TOP: A 1957 OLDSMOBILE GOLDEN ROCKET 88 HOLIDAY SEDAN AT THE SUBURBAN LITTLE LEAGUE GAME ON A TYPICAL SATURDAY IN SPRING.

areas beyond the early suburbs.

Vast new residential communities such as Levittown, Long Island, New York and Daly City, California sprang up virtually overnight, named, of course, for visionary developers such as William Jaird Levitt and John Daly. The homes built by Levitt and Daly were decried for their "cookie-cutter" sameness. A fifties folk song described Daly City as "Little boxes made of ticky-tacky, little boxes on the hillside, little boxes all the same," and added that "there's a green one, and a pink one, and a blue one, and a yellow one, [but] they're all made out of ticky-tacky, and they all look just the same." However, for the returning GIs and their young brides living with their parents in cramped apartments in Brooklyn or San Francisco, the little boxes looked like the doorway to an American dream that would be fulfilled during and by the fifties. The "little boxes" offered the dream of home ownership at reasonable cost and at a reasonable commuting distance from the urban centers. Daly City was just seven miles from the San Francisco Financial District

TOP: OUT FOR A DRIVE. ABOVE: ARRIVING AT SCHOOL, 1958.

and Montgomery Street ("the Wall Street of the West"), while Levittown was only 40 miles east of New York City and the actual Wall Street in Manhattan.

Between 1947 and 1951, William J. Levitt built 17,447 four to five room homes on 6,000-square-foot lots in former potato fields and sold them for around $7,000. Carpenters and masons worked their way up the newly-paved streets like they were as many assembly lines, building over 350 houses a month in what has been called America's "first mass-produced suburb." Levitt also went on to create two more mass-produced suburbs in Pennsylvania and New Jersey. By 1951, when the Long Island project was completed, there were new suburbs being mass produced throughout the United States, notably in California's fast-growing San Fernan-

do Valley in Los Angeles County, a place where suburban culture would reach its apogee by the sixties and which would give rise to the "Valley Girl" culture of the seventies and eighties.

Indeed, the Levitt model would be copied thousands of times in every state and most Canadian provinces, and it would change the face of American culture.

During the fifties, people found their dreams in the suburbs. Urban-style crime was virtually

39

Top: A trip to the mall in the 1959 Edsel.

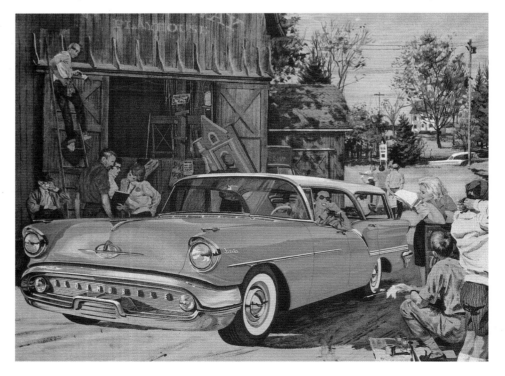

nonexistent. The schools were, for the most part, newer and the teachers seemed to be more energetic. Because the suburbs of the fifties were still largely residential, they were more family-orient-

ed and more home-centered than the fast paced cosmopolitan cities.

The suburbs were also a matriarchal society five days a week as dads commuted to the cities for jobs and moms stayed home in the suburbs, keeping house and caring for the children. Indeed, this stereotype was largely true. During the forties, because of World War II, women had entered the work force in an unprecedented proportion that would not be matched until the late seventies. During the fifties, though, the proportion of women over age 25 in the work force was at roughly the lowest point in the twentieth century. Contrary to the revisionist view, however, the women of the fifties were not prisoners of their suburban homes. With

ABOVE: A VISIT TO THE VILLAGE THEATER IN THE 1957 OLDSMOBILE SUPER 88 FIESTA WAGON. TOP: A GARDENING ACCIDENT.

two cars in the family, or with their husbands travelling to the city by commuter train (which was common in the Northeast and around Chicago), the wives had a mobility that would not have been imagined by previous generations.

Gradually, as the original villages and suburbs grew, the space between them filled in and they became a continuos mass of what came to be decried in the sixties and seventies as "suburban sprawl." However, during the fifties, the lifestyle enjoyed by American suburbanites was as close to perfect as could have been imagined. For that decade at least, suburbs were the embodiment of the American dream. ❋ ❋

41

TOP: *A SHOPPING TRIP FOR SPRINGTIME BEDDING PLANTS IN THE 1955 CHEVROLET BEL AIR.*

DURING THE FIFTIES, COMMUTING FROM THE SUBURBS BECAME A REALITY FOR MILLIONS OF WHITE-COLLAR WORKERS, MOSTLY MEN.

The Fifties Home

The essential fact about the homes of the fifties was that there were simply more of them built than at any previous time in American history. The homes that were built in the fifties were part of a building boom that followed two decades of housing slump, so architecturally they tended to stand out. It was not that people did not want new homes during the thirties and early forties, but in the thirties, during the Depression, they

could not afford a newly-constructed home, or felt ostentatious building one when they knew that their neighbors could not afford a new house. During World War II, new home construction was limited by the wartime need for materials. When the years of repressed demand ended, and the flood of new home buyers hit the marketplace, they wanted something new and often something different.

In the Northeast, home buyers were more traditional and the

44

ABOVE: A WEYERHAEUSER FOUR-SQUARE HOME, 1955.　　OPPOSITE: PLANNING THE NEWLYWEDS' FIRST NEW HOME.

two-story Cape Cod style home with its pitched roof was popular because it represented the type of home that people had been dreaming of. Indeed, William J. Levitt's Levittown consisted of thousands of virtually identical Cape Cods. However, in much of the rest of the United States, the simple, compact ranch-style house was the natur-

al starter home for many young families. The simple, rectangular plan of the ranch-style home, its basic roof structure, and limited number of special details also made it the easiest to build. The ranch-style home was so-called because it was inspired by an idealized image of the rambling, picturesque homes of California and the West.

The operative word was "modern." The definition of this term had evolved since the previous building boom in the twenties, and it held that simplicity and the absence of embellishment were synonymous with "modern." The key to this was the notion that "form follows function," an idea that had come into architectural thought in the twenties by way of the Bauhaus architectural movement in Germany. Form following function meant that the form of an object should be determined by how it is used.

LEFT: PLANNING NEW LIVES FOR NEW FAMILIES.

Since no embellishments or decorative elements add to the function, they should not be added to the form unless they specifically support the function. The Bauhaus architects produced designs that were devoid of what they saw as extraneous and unnecessary decorative elements and reduced design to the minimum necessary to carry the function. The result was something very different and very "clean." Because it was new and not familiar, the Bauhaus look was perceived as "modern." Unfortunately, Bauhaus houses were also very boxlike, and they would ultimately be ridiculed as the "little boxes made of ticky-tacky, little boxes all the same." They were the same, but they were modern. In the fifties, modern was more important than individuality or uniqueness.

One of the artists celebrated by the Bauhaus movement was the Dutch painter Piet Mondrian, whose stark paintings of solid-colored squares and rectangles (usually including the red and blue of the Dutch flag) held together by ladder-like black grids were expressive of the angular simplicity advocated by the Bauhaus. Mondrian died in 1944, but his paintings were incessantly evoked during the fifties in advertising, architec-

47

❋

TOP: NEW BARRETT CAPE COD STYLE HOMES WERE BUILT FOR $12,000 IN THE FIFTIES. OPPOSITE TOP: A WEYERHAEUSER FOUR-SQUARE HOME, 1955.

fifties homes from window grids to the interior room dividers pictured in the following chapters, especially on pages 70-71.

Though it was not a time of widespread home-building, the Bauhaus style, now known as the "International" style, reached the United States in the thirties, where it was embraced by a generation of young architects yearning to make a mark and yearning to be modern. One of the most influential of this generation of "box-builders" was Frank Lloyd Wright, who designed homes with dramatically simplified spaces.

tural detailing and places where "modern" needed to be suggested by a few simple colored panels. The school pictured on page 36 is an excellent example. Mondrian-type patterns are seen in

Historically, it would not be until the late seventies and early eighties that postmodern architecture would revive individuality and complexity as a reaction against the austere Bauhaus style. In the fifties

ABOVE: THIS CHARLES GOODMAN, KELVINATOR-EQUIPPED HOLIDAY HOUSE HAD BAUHAUS SIMPLICITY AND WAS "RIGHT IN TUNE WITH TODAY'S THINKING."

though, simple, clean lines were the definition of modern, and architects were swift to copy Frank Lloyd Wright and his "Bauhausmates."

Beyond being modern, the compact ranch home of the fifties was less expensive to build. It was also practical and it suited the lifestyles of the people of the fifties. Typically, all of the living space was on one level, and with the "old fashioned" stairways completely eliminated, the smaller hallway area got the most from the fewest square feet, saving on cost and embellish-

ment. The simpler, one-story homes also appealed to people who had difficulty climbing stairs.

According to a survey cited by the Barrett Division of Allied Chemical and Dye, who manufactured roofing materials, the second most popular home type in the fifties — behind the ranch-style and ahead of the Cape Cod — was the "modified modern." This house combined the familiar sloped roof with the bold angularity of a Frank Lloyd Wright-inspired purely "modern" box-type home. Also popular during the fifties

49

TOP: A BARRETT HOME WITH DUBLECOTE MULTI-SHINGLES. OPPOSITE TOP: A NEW PICTURE WINDOW WAS ALWAYS A JOY.

were "split level" homes, which had one story, but part of that story was raised a few feet from the main level of the house. While developers such as Bill Levitt and John Daly created huge new towns, firms also sprang up to build and sell pre-fabricated homes. National magazine advertising sold homes that used wartime production techniques to mass produce homes at a central location for shipment to building sites virtually anywhere. Lumber companies such as Weyerhaeuser got into the act, as did firms whose background was specifically in housing construction. In Lafayette, Indiana, the National Homes Corporation, which began in 1940, grew dramatically in response to the need for wartime housing. By the fifties, National Homes was the nation's largest builder of prefabricated housing. Their popular slogan was simply that "Better Homes Build a Better America."

New materials also came into play. Whereas the prewar homes where the parents of the baby

ABOVE: DAD COMES HOME TO INSPECT THE NEW JOHNS-MANVILLE SIDING. TOP: HELPING OUT IN DAD'S SHOP.

HOMES PRESENTS THE 1954 "RANGER" SERIES OF...

Breath-Taking New Nationals

for modern living...for any income!

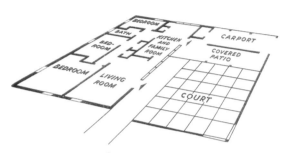

Your every desire for abundant and relaxed living is fulfilled in this, the newest of the 1954 Nationals.

Here is sheltered indoor and outdoor living at its best, with a secluded garden court and a glass-walled family room for your informal living and recreation, shielded from the rest of the world.

Truly, the "Ranger" opens a new era in family life. And National makes it a home *you* can own. Our illustrated brochure tells you more. Ask your nearest National dealer-builder for a copy or write National Homes Corporation, Dept. LF5, Lafayette, Indiana. Do it today.

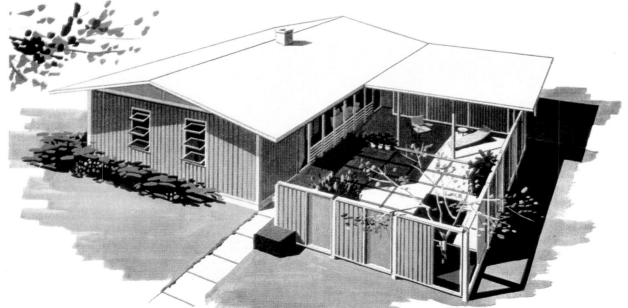

A WORLD-FAMOUS ARCHITECT, Charles M. Goodman, AIA, created the stunning new designs for 1954 Nationals. He says, "I consider National Homes the greatest single force for progress in home building today."

NOW—AIR CONDITIONED! National Homes research brings you complete air conditioning for all models, at unbelievably low cost — as low as $500 additional!

BETTER HOMES BUILD A BETTER AMERICA

National HOMES®

NATIONAL HOMES CORPORATION
LAFAYETTE, INDIANA • HORSEHEADS, N. Y.

National Homes prefabricated panels and structural parts as they leave the assembly plant carry the Good Housekeeping guarantee seal and Parents' Magazine seal of commendation.

Hear GABRIEL HEATTER..."Good News Today"... Mutual Network, every Monday, Wednesday and Friday morning!

boomers grew up had wooden siding, the houses of the fifties often had aluminum or asbestos siding. While asbestos was discredited in the seventies because of the potential for lung damage, it was extremely popular in the fifties because of the fear of home fires.

The amenities offered in these modern homes included central heating, as well as central air conditioning, and some even had central vacuum cleaning systems, a feature that persists to this day, though it has never really caught on like central heating did. One important feature that especially characterized the homes of the fifties was the picture window. Large panels, often consisting of 15 to 20 square feet of tempered, high strength glass, afforded broad, uninterrupted vis-

ABOVE: THE TWO-CAR FAMILY ENJOYED UNPRECEDENTED FREEDOM IN THEIR LEISURE ACTIVITIES. TOP: THE DISHWASHER WAS IMPORTANT TO THE FIFTIES HOME.

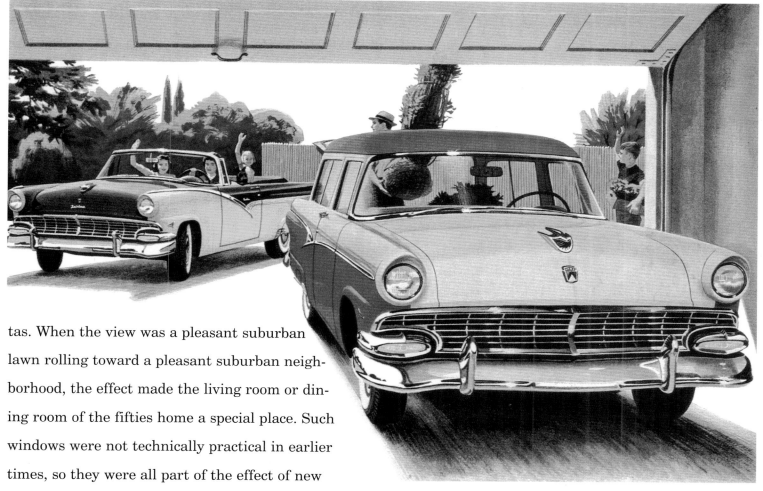

tas. When the view was a pleasant suburban lawn rolling toward a pleasant suburban neighborhood, the effect made the living room or dining room of the fifties home a special place. Such windows were not technically practical in earlier times, so they were all part of the effect of new homes in the fifties being different than their predecessors. Of course, many people with older homes had picture windows retrofitted into their houses, but these almost never looked as natural as they did in a home built after 1950.

Finally, many homes constructed after 1950 had that symbol of prosperity that was virtually unthinkable in a middle class home from an earlier time. This was the two-car garage. Once a two-car garage had symbolized affluence. In the fifties, however, the two-car garage represented not only the general prosperity of the times, but also the newly-found mobility of the suburban middle class. ✳ ✳

53

TOP: IN THE FIFTIES, HOMES WERE ROUTINELY BUILT WITH TWO-CAR GARAGES. IN 1956, FORD TARGET-MARKETED ITS CARS TO TWO-CAR FAMILIES.

We scouted 42 states to find these matchless houses near Cleveland, Ohio ... beautiful, efficient, yet economical. And what a perfect setting! Ridgewood Country Club Homes are built by the Par Construction Company on the edge of a rolling, wooded golf course! Our experts commend this home builder for excellent design, sound construction and the use of famous brand names. We show some of these well-known products on this page.

Model house now open at
6385 W. 54th Street,
Parma 29, Ohio.

these houses TOP them all

We've never seen such a beautifully *luminous* roof color. It's achieved with new Ruberoid BLUE-GLO asphalt shingles ... an exclusive blend of blues, greens, reds, white and buff that gives the roof a soft, deep, youthful look ... good for years. Here, we say, is the latest in home styles, featured by many style-minded builders and roofing specialists. They're Ruberoid Lok-Tab® asphalt shingles: they *defy* wind; interlocking tabs *lock* the shingles tightly together. With a Lok-Tab roof you get Ruberoid's exclusive Written Warranty against blow-offs! ... **Ruberoid.**

Talk about famous brand names...and you are bound to say Formica®! Here is the "Show Kitchen" of our Show House ... made forever new with eye-pleasing "Nassau" counter-tops by Formica. Genuine Formica laminated plastic surfaces—for walls, work tops, furniture—are a joy ... they *stay* beautiful. And you have your pick of colors and patterns from Formica *dozens*. Look in the Yellow Pages under "Plastics" for a Formica fabricator. Send coupon for the big Formica Decorating Idea Book for $1.00 or free color literature. **Formica**

Home builders buy smart! They know quality. They know that's why so many now use Armstrong ... world's finest heating equipment. Armstrong gives *more*. More comfort —the exclusive "Quiet Fire" burner in our Armstrong Lo-Hi-Boy Furnace (right) provides silent, safe and sure heat. More experience—Armstrong has devoted thirty years to the manufacture of home comfort. More service—Armstrong equipment is designed and built for the years. Air conditioning can be added now or later. See coupon for helpful literature on ... **Armstrong.**

Here's our amazing "scrubless" kitchen! You never have to scrub Crown Vinyl by Sandran. This *heavy duty* floor covering with a solid 100% vinyl wear layer comes clean instantly with one swish of a damp mop. It doesn't need constant waxing because it has a built-in gleam ... resists scuffing, too! Stainmakers (lye, grapejuice, even grease) that stain ordinary floor coverings won't stain Crown Vinyl by Sandran. We show several lovely patterns. It's the only floor covering we know of with a *12-year* Beauty-Wear Guarantee. Low cost, too! **Sandran**

At last! Smart new bathroom beauty: Borg-Warner's Ingersoll-Humphryes Plumbing Fixtures in HOUSE & GARDEN colors. Here, in Citron Yellow, are a unique tub (with raised bottom, and wide, safe apron seat) ... a handsome new lavatory ... and, best of all, the sensational new wall-hung toilet! *Up, off the floor,* this luxurious, spacesaver (with tank concealed in the wall) is so quiet and sanitary...so easy to clean around and under — and to keep clean. **Ingersoll-Humphryes Div., BORG-WARNER. Since 1882.**

A basement planned for living! The latest thing in well-designed new homes made possible by Bilco, America's finest basement door. All steel for permanence ... weather tight ... attractive ... operates at a touch. With a Bilco you are only a few steps to a gardener's haven, a well-equipped and safe recreation room and hobby shop. Bilco supplements interior stairs keeping unnecessary traffic out of first floor rooms. Amazing improvement for your present home, too, a Bilco is the modern replacement for your wood hatchway. Sold by building material dealers. Send coupon. **The Bilco Co.**

SHOW-HOUSE
TO BETTER YOUR HOME LIVING

...er 22 in a series of advertisements by SHOW-HOUSE, 555 Fifth Ave., N. Y. 17.

TOPS in quality...TOPS in value

...TWORK: ELDRIDGE KING

A custom community, Lake Isle Estates — created by famous builder Allan V. Rose — wins our praise for a truly majestic and picturesque site. Think of it—mountain woodlands and lakes just 34 minutes from Manhattan's Towers! These quality homes in Westchester County border and overlook beautiful Lake Innisfree. Mr. Rose offers home buyers the utmost in quality and value...below we illustrate a few of the outstanding products seen in the model home. If you live in the New York City area, why not see the *goodness* of Lake Isle Estates for yourself.

Model house now open at Lake Shore Drive, Eastchester, New York.

The Mutschler cabinets in our kitchen are as beautifully built as your best furniture. Mutschler, in fact, insists they *are* furniture . . . and we heartily agree. For here you'll find a glowing natural finish, solid hardware, careful joinery. It's an efficient kitchen, too, with stacks of drawers, shelving, and flowing worktops. We have seen many kitchens. This Mutschler kitchen is one of the best. It highlights this group of *new* homes; it can rejuvenate your *present* one. Check our coupon . . . **Mutschler.**

Our Westinghouse Under-Counter Dishwasher wastes nary an inch of counter top. It's big: handles service for 10! It's full of special features you'll find nowhere else: its own exclusive Water Temperature Monitor protects your health . . . guarantees 140° *hot* water for sanitary-clean dishes. Choose from 15 fronts... 5 colors, 7 wood fronts, 2 metallic finishes (we show Antique Copper), and ready-to-paint steel. Our Food Waste Disposer is cushion-quiet; disposes of all food waste—even bones. **You can be SURE . . . if it's Westinghouse.**

...ntroducing, *new* ceramic ...ile color—Regency Blue ...y Stylon...a truly *famous* ...rand name. Famous for ...exture and color, famous ...or quality—that's Stylon. ...nd in these famous ...omes, we use Stylon ...eramic tile *exclusively* in ...ll bathrooms. On the ...oor, another SHOW-...HOUSE first: 12" x 12" ...Crystal-Glaze ceramic ...le by Stylon. And on ...he counter, smaller ...quares of the same. Per-...nanence, easy mainte-...ance, sheer beauty . . . ...rought to you by Stylon. ...galaxy of new ceramic ...le ideas are featured in ...he Stylon literature our ...oupon offers . . . **Stylon.**

Pella windows add excitement to our Show-House! Care-free PELLA MULTI-PURPOSE WINDOWS with self-storing screens serve both the living room in the foreground and the dining area adjoining. PELLA CASEMENT WINDOWS with *screens that roll up and down* can be seen in the family room and they are also in the bathroom and bedrooms. New PELLA TWINLITE WINDOWS over kitchen sink open out like "awnings." All are available with insulating glass. The PELLA WOOD FOLDING DOOR, at right, blends handsomely with fine wood furnishings. **Pella.®**

Hidden quality! This home builder puts quality into his homes . . . "beyond the eye." Naturally, he uses modern Bermico Bituminized Fibre Pipe for house-to-sewer connections because it is dependable, root-proof, trouble-free . . . and it is made to last and last. This means that *you*, Mr. and Mrs. Home Owner, will have *complete* satisfaction. Be sure to look "beyond the eye" for Bermico when you build or remodel your house . . . or visit a model home: Bermico and *good* builders go together! Use our coupon for two valuable booklets by **Bermico.**

clip this helpful coupon...

SHOW-HOUSE, Box 1500, Grand Central Sta., N. Y. 17, N. Y. Please send me the better living aids checked below. I enclose coins (no stamps) to cover the cost of those for which there is a charge.

1. RUBEROID: □ Free color folder showing decorator-designed Lok-Tabs and □ "High Fashion" Auto-claved Sidewalls.
2. ARMSTRONG: □ "Home Heating Has Changed, Too" . . . better heating for every house. □ "New World of Comfort" how to get economical air conditioning.
3. BORG-WARNER CORP.: □ Free Folder: Ingersoll-Humphryes plumbing fixtures.
4. FORMICA: □ Decorating Idea Book, $1.00. □ New colorful literature—free.
5. SANDRAN: □ Free booklet and samples to help you plan an Amazing "Scrubless" Kitchen.
6. BILCO: □ Literature for new home builders,

□ "How-To-Do-It": folder for replacing wood door.
7. MUTSCHLER: □ Kitchen Literature, 10¢.
8. STYLON TILE: □ Full color catalog showing the latest colors and patterns in ceramic tile, 10¢.
9. BERMICO: □ Complete Bermico Catalog, □ How and Where to Install a Septic Tank System, 25¢.
10. WESTINGHOUSE: □ Color literature on Automatic Dishwashers and Food Waste Disposers, 10¢.
11. PELLA: □ Multi-Purpose Windows, □ Casement Windows, □ Twinlite Windows, □ Window Idea Book, 25¢, □ Wood Folding Doors.
12. □ Architect's Blue-Plans of both houses, including builder's descriptive brochure, 25¢

This coupon good until April 25, 1958. Please print name and address. (Allow 3-4 weeks for delivery.)

In The Kitchen

The fifties were a special moment for kitchens because there was probably no other time in history — before or since — when more people bought appliances. As with so many other things about the fifties, there were myriad changes because of both technology and pent-up demand for something new. Perhaps nowhere in the home of the fifties were improvements in technology more apparent than in the kitchen. Not only were

pre-fifties appliances old in terms of technology, they were, or appeared, just plain *old*.

The "all-electric" kitchen became the last word in "modern" during the fifties, because many people were well aware that many rural parts of the United States did not have electricity until the thirties, and some of them were not electrified until the forties.

During World War II, appliances had not been manufactured, and it took

56

✳

industry some time to gear up for mass production, so in most kitchens of the late forties, most appliances were eight to ten years old. Beyond that, during the Depression, most people replaced appliances only when they were broken beyond repair, so that pushed the average age of appliances even higher.

Today it is easy to forget that before the fifties, the types of appliances that we take for granted in our kitchens today were not exactly ubiquitous. In fact, almost everybody of voting age in the late forties had distinct memories of the days when refrigerators were literally *ice boxes*. Modern refrigerators were not mass produced until the early twenties, and the first models were only about ten years old when the Depression began, and many of them were still in place in the late forties. It was 1939 when General Electric had introduced the familiar two-compartment refrigerator with the separate freezer compartment, and relatively few had been sold when production was curtailed by the war effort. By the mid-fifties, those people who had grown up with a memory of true ice boxes were able to buy refrigerators that made ice cubes automatically.

Frigidaire, proudly touting itself as "America's No. 1 Refrigerator," offered four series in ten sizes, with Lifetime Porcelain or Durable Dulux exteriors. They came in sizes

58

LEFT: *DELIGHTED WITH HER NEW KELVINATOR.*

that ranged from four to 17 cubic feet and up to 70 pounds of frozen storage area. The look and styling of the new appliances was also of extreme importance. Just as the homes themselves were becoming architecturally modern, the appliances had to look as though they were not just a stepchild of prewar designs. Leading industrial designers were employed. Frigidaire even went so far as to enlist the services of Raymond Loewy, the dean of American industrial design. It has been said that to a degree unequaled by the names of any of the other founding fathers of industrial design, the name of Raymond Loewy radiates a charisma that has attracted public attention throughout the second half of the twentieth century. Loewy's highly developed imagination and rich design talent was an important element in generating a sense of excitement about

many postwar products. Loewy's design philosophy was summarized with the acronym MAYA (most advanced, yet acceptable). The proliferation of clean, functional, and dynamic products that emerged from the Loewy offices throughout

59

TOP: *A COLORFUL GENERAL ELECTRIC BH-15 FOR 1957 HAD A MAGNETIC SAFETY DOOR AND A 175-POUND ROLL-OUT FREEZER.*

his long career provides testimony to his success. Among his designs were the Coca-Cola bottle, and the famous 1947 Studebaker Starlight Coupe and 1953 Starliner Coupe, designs that generated a public interest and acceptance far out of proportion to Studebaker's relative size in the automotive industry. Loewy also designed the trademarks for Shell, Exxon, Armour, International Harvester, Pepsodent and Lucky Strike.

Frigidaire may have had Raymond Loewy, but General Electric's LH-12 12-cubic-foot refrigerator-freezer, marketed in 1956, had revolving shelves to make things easy to reach. General Electric also bragged about the LH-12's "magnetic safety doors." Now legally mandated, magnetic safety doors were in response to several well-publicized stories in the fifties about small children being trapped inside refrigerators.

International Harvester, a builder of trucks and farm machinery, got into the rapidly expanding refrigerator market in the early fifties with refrigerators that were "*femineered*," meaning engineered for women. The slogan said of International Harvester refrigerators, "Women dreamed them. . . home economists designed them." The implication was that refrigerators were the subject of women's dreams and that men didn't use refrigerators. While the femi-

60

nists of the seventies would have bristled at these statements, in the fifties it really was true that women ran the kitchens and their husbands rarely came to call except at midnight snack time.

Crosley also played to the notion of refrigerators being a woman's appliance with its Shelvador, which was "designed from the woman's angle." What angle that was is not really explained in Crosley advertising, but women *were* told: "You just wouldn't be human if you didn't want to show off your beautiful new Shelvador." What the Crosley Shelvador actually offered was "sturdy, snow-white plastic shelves, completely recessed into the door," as well as lift out shelves and transparent crispers. Why a *man* could not appreciate these features is not known.

As the vast new housing developments were being built, clean, modern kitchens were an essential selling point, and at the time, "clean" meant all-electric. Between 1947 and 1951 as William J. Levitt was building the 17,447 four to five room homes that would comprise the legendary Levittown on Long Island, he specifically installed steel kitchen cabinets, a Bendix washing

TOP: THE CROSLEY SHELVADOR WITH THE SHELVES IN THE DOOR WAS "DESIGNED FROM THE WOMAN'S ANGLE."

machine, a General Electric refrigerator, and a Hotpoint electric range.

Sales of electric appliances increased dramatically during the fifties, reaching a peak during 1955 and 1956. While sales of appliances had been virtually nil in 1945, wartime scarcity was followed by an appliance buying binge that crested in 1955. In that year alone 4.2 million refrigerators, 1.4 million electric ranges and 1.1 million home freezers were sold.

Kelvinator offered a double oven electric range with "Automatic Cook" controls that allowed a housewife to cook an entire meal at once. It has a low setting that allowed chocolate to be melted in the wrapper and a "Rocket" set-

ting that heated to red hot in seconds. Crosley, when introducing the 1951 "Electric Range with Beauty and Brains," proudly asserted that it was the "Cooking miracle of '51 that does everything automatically." What it had was the type of combination clock and timer that is now common on ranges and microwave ovens. Of course, in 1951, the Crosley controls were electro-mechanical rather than electronic.

General Electric's Stratoliner range, which was named for a Boeing airliner, had a lighted control panel that was worthy of an airliner. Its Tel-A-Cook system had push-buttons (push-buttons were a very popular feature in the appliances of the fifties), and different colored lights to

LEFT: ADVERTISING THE CAN-O-MAT OF 1958.

show what was cooking. An automatic oven timer allowed General Electric to say that "Dinner cooks by itself!"

Sales of built-in electric ranges, a new innovation in the early fifties, soared from $57 million to $107 million between 1955 and 1956, and went up another ten percent in 1957. Sales of clothes dryers, another innovation that was a key part of the fifties home and lifestyle, reached $217 million in 1955 and soared to $252 million in 1956. Portable mixers, another appliance that was virtually unavailable prior to the fifties, became suddenly very popular, with sales reaching $32 million in 1955 and $49 million at the peak in 1956.

Dishwashers were a labor saving device that found themselves the crown jewels of fifties kitchens. Kitchen Aid, whose basic design would endure through the end of the century, spoke to

women in a quiet tone when it asked its 1957 advertising: "Actually you're the same person you were when you married — you still like to go places together. . . do the things you used to do. . . or maybe ask somebody over — but what to do with those everlasting stacks of dirty dishes?"

63

✳

TOP: THE O'KEEFE & MERRITT GAS RANGE AND SERVEL GAS REFRIGERATOR HAD THE CLEANLINESS OF ELECTRIC APPLIANCES AND "PERFECT" CONTROLS.

Kitchen Aid then offered to "take over — automatically" and give the housewife the opportunity to enjoy life with her husband. The implication was that she should also not ask him to help her do the dishes. Dishwashers continued to sell in large numbers through the decade. American consumers spent $90 million on dishwashers in 1955, and $116 million in 1956. Meanwhile, though, they spent almost as much ($113 million

in 1956) on electric skillets, a particularly fifties innovation that is rarely used today.

Technical features aside, the era of prosperity that prevailed during the fifties also made the home and kitchen an exciting environment. In these new kitchens, the homemakers of the fifties fashioned meals that were a blend of what they had learned from *their* mothers, from women's magazines and from swapping recipes with friends across the back yard fence. Grandma's time-tested favorites were still a staple, but mom was willing to try something new from the spice drawer once in a while.

The fifties were really the golden age of American *home* cooking. The new kitchens allowed the young housewives to cook the recipes they had learned from their mothers and grandmothers with ease, and the unprecedented array of labor-saving kitchen appliances gave them time to experiment a little bit without straying too far from the basics. The fifties were an era

LEFT: THE GENERAL ELECTRIC STRATOLINER RANGE FOR 1950.

when packaged foods meant canned peas. The concept of entire packaged meals (then called "TV dinners") was invented in the fifties, but few people resorted to these more than once a week until the sixties.

In the fifties, we saw the meals that mom put on the table as being truly American. In the sixties, when "foreign" food, such as pizza, started to be common, a typical comment was that the only two foreign foods most people had ever tasted were Swiss cheese and French fries. It is certainly true that the American diets were much more limited then. Almost no one had ever tasted a taco, and pizza was something that you could find only in the Italian neighborhoods of larger cities. Terminology was also different. The word "pasta" had not yet entered our vocabulary. Noodles were noodles, and macaroni came with elbows or it came shaped like the letters in our "alphabet" soup.

However limited they may have been, the basic foods were better back then. A home-made hot dish is *always* better than anything that you find pre-packaged in the frozen food section. The fifties were the wonderful days of bean salad, baked beans and green bean casseroles.

65

TOP: IN THE FIFTIES, A MODERN KITCHEN OFTEN HAD PLENTY OF SPARKLING STAINLESS STEEL.

Often adjacent to the kitchen in the new homes built during the fifties was the home laundry. Washing machines had been in general use for a generation, but automatic dryers were the major washday innovation of the fifties. Clotheslines were standard equipment at every single-family home in North America. As late as the mid-fifties, you could drive through a small town or suburb on any sunny day and see back yard clotheslines covered with billowing sheets and apparel. The emphasis here is, of course, on *sunny day*. Housewives were traditionally at the mercy of the weather when doing the wash because wind and rain were the enemies of line drying. All too common was the image of a poor housewife frantically pulling clothes off the line as the first raindrops of a storm pounded her forehead. Kelvinator even used the phrase "bring June into your home" to advertise its automatic dryer. Among the home appliances that truly earned the name "modern convenience," the clothes dryer was at the head of the list.

Washing machines also went through many important changes in the fifties. Indeed, it was during that decade that most of the

LEFT: THE GENERAL ELECTRIC DRYER FOR 1958.

improvements we see in today's machines occurred. Washing machines changed dramatically in the fifties, and have changed little since. At the beginning of the decade, the wash often came out of the machine with soap scum, and the aggravating problem of balls of lint in one's socks was infuriating. General Electric's Filter-Flo system, announced in 1956, solved this problem with a filter that was inserted atop the agitator.

With dryers, there were many changes. Snagging inside the drying drum was overcome, as was the annoyance of having lint and dust spew out of the machine. The problem of the dryer being too hot at one point was resolved by Maytag's 1959 "Halo of Heat" system.

By the late fifties, automatic controls had become standard on both washers and dryers, so that timing was no longer a problem. In 1959, General Electric introduced the separate setting control for normal, delicate and heavy that is common today. The same year, Whirlpool announced a "revolution in automatic drying" with its Automatic Fabric Control and its Moisture Minder, which "sensed" when the clothes were dry enough. Norge, meanwhile, billed its Dispensomat Washer as "the world's first *truly*

67

✳

TOP: THE WESTINGHOUSE LAUNDRAMAT AUTOMATIC WASHER OF 1951 WAS THE HARBINGER OF GREAT NEW APPLIANCES TO COME.

automatic washer." It had a console with not only machine controls, but separate bays for inserting detergent, bleach, fabric softener and water conditioner. The modern console, like the dashboard of a fifties car, was heavily chromed and it even had a clock.

The fifties also saw the beginning of the convention of selling matched washer-dryer sets, in which both machines, although separate units, were the same height and available in matching

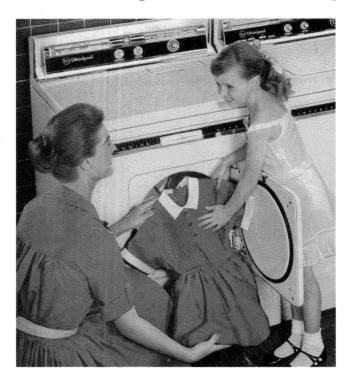

colors. Because gas was still preferred by many for drying, dryers were available — as they are to this day — in either gas or electric.

As the new appliances went in, the kitchens themselves were remodeled. People put new linoleum or congoleum on their floors and walls and redecorated with the new colors of the fifties, such as pinks and turquoises. Linoleum was the signature artificial flooring of the early fifties, but it would gradually be superceded by more durable plastics. It was not a new product in 1950. In fact, it was invented in England in 1863 by Frederick Walton, who coined the name linoleum from the Latin name, *linum*, which means flax, and *oleum*, which means oil. Later in the century, Michael Nairn, a flooring manufacturer in Kirkcaldy, Scotland perfected the flooring, introducing qualities such as inlaid patterning. Linoleum is manufactured by oxidizing linseed oil to form a thick mixture called linoleum cement. The cement is cooled and mixed with

LEFT: THE 1958 WHIRLPOOL DRYER WITH MOISTURE MINDER.

See these spots disappear in 60 seconds with the "MAGIC MINUTE"!

Only the new 1957 Kelvinator Washer brings you the
"Magic Minute"

60 SECONDS OF AUTOMATIC PRE-SCRUBBING WITH DOUBLE-RICH SUDS TO CUT GREASE BETTER, WASH EVERYTHING CLEANER

GIVE YOUR toughest washing problems to the "Magic Minute"—an entirely new kind of automatic washing by Kelvinator.

SPILL GREASE on a pretty apron. Splash it with coffee. Smear it with meat sauce. Then watch the new 1957 Kelvinator go to work.

Kelvinator starts with the "Magic Minute"—60 seconds of automatic pre-scrubbing with the full amount of soap and only a small amount of water. This cuts grease and grime *before* the regular washing action starts.

Following the "Magic Minute" the tub fills completely and the "3-Way Agitator" washes out every last speck of dirt. No other washing action gets clothes so white, so bright!

Kelvinator has 2 separate automatic cycles—one for regular fabrics, one for fine fabrics. "Suds Back" for suds and water economy. New push-button control gives a choice of water temperatures. There are no gears to get out of order and cause service problems. Ask your Kelvinator dealer to demonstrate the "Magic Minute".

69

DIVISION OF AMERICAN MOTORS CORPORATION
Detroit 32, Michigan

Kelvinator Super-Speed, Triple-Safe Dryer dries clothes as fast as they are washed. And it's the only dryer with these three big safety features: *Safe Temperatures; Safe Cylinder; Safety Door.* Matching washer and dryer are available in three customer-approved colors or white.

LEFT: DAD IS "DRESSED FOR DINNER," WHILE MOM WHIPS UP BREAKFAST IN HER STAINLESS STEEL PAN ON HER DOUBLE-OVEN FLORENCE ELECTRIC RANGE. MOM AND SIS ARE DRESSED FORMALLY BY TODAY'S STANDARDS, BUT IN THE FIFTIES, THESE WERE EVERYDAY CLOTHES. DAD USUALLY DIDN'T DRESS QUITE THIS FORMALLY. WITH ITS VINYL STOOLS, THIS MODERN BREAKFAST AREA WAS TYPICAL OF THE FIFTIES.

BELOW: A VERY TYPICAL EARLY FIFTIES KITCHEN WITH MODERN FURNITURE, A CLEAN, NEW, SIMPLIFIED ROOM DIVIDER, GOLD SEAL VINYLTOP COUNTERS AND A GOLD SEAL VINYLFLOR WITH INLAID VINYL. SUCH FLOORS TOOK HARD WEAR AND SCUFFING BETTER THAN CONTEMPORARY LINOLEUM.

pine resin, and fine sawdust to form sheets on a jute backing. The term linoleum is often used incorrectly to describe any sheet flooring, when in fact flooring can be made from other materials, such as polyvinyl chloride.

By the end of the decade, manufacturers finally started offering kitchen and home laundry appliances in colors — at no extra cost — as well.

General Electric's palette of canary yellow, petal pink, turquoise green and cadet blue were typical, but white continued in the line with many manufacturers. Although it appeared during the fifties in upholstery fabric, avocado green would be a sixties color in the kitchen. In

71

✳

retrospect, one wonders why, if "new" and "modern" were so important in the early fifties, most appliances remained available only in white for most of the decade. Even Raymond Loewy designed his early fifties Frigidares in institutional white, although he did highlight the interiors with "Ice-Blue" trim.

During the fifties, the familiar, but no longer beloved, old wooden kitchen cabinets were replaced by gleaming metal ones that were enameled in bright, modern colors. Sleek metal and plastic dining room and breakfast nook furniture replaced the old stuff that had been handed down for a generation or two. The clean, mod-

ABOVE: IN 1952, TRADITIONAL KITCHENS COULD BE "DRESSED UP" WITH A NEW FLOOR, ROOM DIVIDER AND DUCO ENAMEL ON THE OLD CABINETS.

ern kitchens that were built for housing developments such as Levittown were designed with steel rather than wood cabinets.

Stainless steel in the kitchen was viewed as a major lifestyle change. Republic Steel admonished husbands to "Surround her with stainless . . . she'll love it for life! Happy is the wife with a household of stainless steel ware and appliances. Party-pretty stainless is starring on the smartest tables and best-run kitchens. Stainless is fashion-right, stays lifelong bright. She loves not polishing stainless, but using it and enjoying it. Stainless resists tarnishing; resists rust and corrosion; has no applied surface to chip, peel or wear away [as nickel or chrome plating on steel often did.] It is superbly easy to clean and keep clean. So sanitary! No polishing, no pampering needed. She has more time for children, for clubs, for garden, for fun, for you."

Allegheny Ludlum Steel, it its publication *Stainless for Living*, asked: "When you say something is modern in design, you mean more than just new, don't you? You mean that it's not only beautiful, but practical. Simplified, not fancy. Functional. Work-saving. Economical."

Stainless for Living read like a Bauhaus manifesto, but Bauhaus and stainless were "modern." This was what people wanted in the fifties. This was the fifties kitchen. ✳ ✳

73

✳

The Living Room

During the fifties, the family living room was the family's showcase. It was the room that was always presented to guests who came to call, and the way it was decorated was expressive of the image that a family wished to project. In many homes, the living room was also known as the "front" room. The living room was also the place that the family itself often gathered, mom and dad in their favorite chairs, and the

kids playing quietly on the floor or watching television. In the seventies and early eighties, the living room would be sealed off, a mere showcase, while the actual "living" took place in a room called a "family room." However, in the fifties, the living room was for living and it was where the family lived.

That which was shown in this showcase room was that which was shown by the house itself. It made a statement, and

RIGHT: LIGHT WOOD AND VIVID PAINT.

OPPOSITE: ENJOYING THE LIVING ROOM.

74

✳

that statement was usually *modern*. While period furniture, such as regency and French provincial remained somewhat popular, the new modern looks would predominate. People who were living in an older home or who could not afford to remodel, could and would use their living room to express their rejection of the old Victorian look of their grandparents or the art deco or twenties look toward which their parents had gravitated. The "modern" look of the fifties was a look that had existed in some of the smart uptown apartments of the late thirties and forties, but with the return of peace and prosperity after World War II, it was now making its way to Main Street in big crates being unloaded from moving vans at every corner.

In terms of tangible design features, the modern look of the fifties was simple and practical. The upholstered furniture, for example, was squared and angular, rejecting the comfortable "roll-arm" look that had been popular throughout the first half of the twentieth century.

ABOVE: A TYPICAL LATE FIFTIES LIVING ROOM WITH BRIGHT PASTELS. TOP: TYPICAL EARLY FIFTIES COLORS WERE DARKER. CLEAN STYLING IS SEEN IN BOTH.

The furniture of the fifties resembled the furniture designed a generation earlier at the Bauhaus and clearly embodied the cornerstone Bauhaus principal that "form follows function." Indeed, this principal is often described in the context of furniture. At the Bauhaus, they used the illustration of a chair: Since its function is to support a sitting person, it should be little more than a horizontal surface and a vertical surface on a frame. Since no embellishments or decorative elements add to the function, they should not be added to the form. At the Bauhaus, as in the furniture factories of the upper Midwest and the Carolinas in the fifties, designers stripped away the extraneous, unnecessary decorative elements and reduced design to the minimum necessary for the function. Colorful fabrics were often used, but the lines of the furniture itself were

77

TOP: MAKING MUSIC TOGETHER WAS BOTH A CAUSE AND EFFECT OF THE FAMILY COHESIVENESS FOR WHICH THE FIFTIES ARE REMEMBERED.

very clean and straightforward. Florence Knoll's parallel bar and rivet construction achieved a slim and delicate look in a remarkably strong basic structure. This look would characterize much of the fifties look, even after 1957, when curves and softer contours would enjoy a limited resurgence. Indeed, it will be remembered that the "look of 1959" was the so-called "thin look," which had extremely straight lines and sharp corners.

Early in the fifties, lighter colored woods, such as birch and ash, came into vogue, superceding the dark, heavy look of mahogany and dark stained oak that had been popular since the Victorian era. Neutral tones were popular not only in wood, but in accent pieces, such as table lamps. With upholstery, how-

ever, bright colors, such as blues and deep, true reds and purples, were quite fashionable, replacing the more subtle earth tones of the forties.

78

ABOVE: A VERY TYPICAL EARLY SIXTIES LIVING ROOM, WITH SLEEK MODERN SHELVING, TABLES, LAMPS AND ACCENTS.

Whereas living room furniture had always been wood or upholstered wood, new materials that had been developed during World War II became available. These included lucite, acrylics, polyester resins, fiberglass, and foam rubber. The furniture makers of the fifties also used the emerging technologies of wood lamination and arc welding. Plywood furniture, previously unthinkable except as something for the kids in the back yard, became popular when the means were developed to form it into contoured shapes.

Meanwhile, the colored, molded fiberglass chair, invented by Charles Eames in 1950, became a fifties icon. In 1958, industrial designer Donald Deskey introduced his famous laminated plastic chair — available in blue and burnt sienna — that is remembered as one of the most widely used chairs of the decade, albeit mainly in institutional settings. The so-called "invisible

THE KROEHLER SECTIONAL SOFA HAD "CUSHIONIZED" CONSTRUCTION AND METALLIC NYLON FABRICS IN "EXCITING NEW COLORS."

79

chair," constructed of translucent lucite, made its appearance in 1959, setting the stage for the "space age bachelor pad" look of the early sixties.

A a harbinger of a wave of Scandinavian furniture trends that would sweep into the market in the late fifties, Finnish designer Eero Saarinen created the "tulip" pedestal chair in 1956, which was manufactured by Knoll Associates. It was ahead of its time, but, in general, Scandinavian furniture, especially the solid, lighter wood pieces from Denmark, became very popular after 1956.

Beginning in about 1957, the Spanish look began to have an influence, and this tended to bring back darker wood tones. Meanwhile, dark lacquers, including black, came into fashion when the "Oriental" look attained wide acceptance in the late fifties. The Oriental styles, either imported or manufactured in America, enjoyed a strong popularity, especially on the West Coast.

ABOVE: A 1956 "ORIENTAL-STYLE" LIVING ROOM WITH SLEEK, MODERN FURNITURE, A JADE GREEN PALETTE AND ARMSTRONG TEXTELLE LINOLEUM.

In furnishing a new home in the fifties, only kitchen appliances came ahead of the "living room set." A typical living room set in the early fifties consisted of an upholstered couch or sofa and a pair of matching upholstered chairs. A set of matching end tables with a matching coffee table would also be added. Later in the decade, living room sets might substitute a multi-piece sectional for the single sofa. Simmons introduced the Hide-A-Bed, a sofa that folded out into a bed, and these were popular, especially with people in smaller "starter" homes.

New furniture of types that had not existed prior to the fifties was almost invariably modern, with straightforward lines and simplified contours. Among the pieces that had had not existed before the fifties were such items as television consoles and hi-fi cabinets. Homes had radio cabinets in the thirties and forties, and these were quickly replaced by the newer electronic gear. The new technology, like the older radios, generally came as a nicely styled piece of furniture, rather than simply as a component such as we see today. The living room was still a semi-formal environment, and it was not a place where the lady of the house would want to have the odd

81

TOP: VERY ORIENTAL STYLING CHARACTERIZES THIS MODERN 1955 HOME DONE WITH A CORKSTONE KENFLEX FLOOR.

piece of hardware sitting on the shelf. Portable record players did exist, but these were typically owned by teenagers, who used them in their bedrooms. Radios and the new clock-radios also came as smaller components, and these were seen only in the kitchen, the bedroom or in dad's workshop out in the garage.

In terms of the new electronics, the high fidelity record player, or simply "the hi-fi" was an important part of family life in the fifties. It was not as important as the television, but certainly it was a "must have" item. The 12-inch vinyl 33 rpm long-playing phonograph record (LP) had been introduced in 1947. Because of the high fidelity sound quality, it was a dramatic improvement over 78 rpm records, and people began to purchase hi-fi record players to replace their old 78 rpm machines. Later in the fifties, as stereophonic records became widely available, they too were pressed as 12-inch vinyl 33 rpm LPs, and

the makers of hi-fi as furniture quickly adapted their products with the necessary electronics to accommodate the two-channel stereophonic sound. The seven-inch 45 rpm records also appeared, but these contained only two songs. These were

LEFT: THE MAGNAVOX CONTINENTAL HI-FI.

bought by teenagers who played them on the smaller, portable record players in their bedrooms, although they were playable on the larger living room consoles.

Another piece of furniture that was increasingly popular in the fifties was the reclining chair, particularly the BarcaLounger. This recliner was manufactured by the company of the same name, which was founded in 1940 when Edward Joel Barcolo acquired a license to manufacture "scientifically articulated" motion chairs that had been patented by Dr. Anton Lorenz.

The typical day in a typical fifties living room followed a predictable pattern. In the morning, the living room was usually empty, as the family gathered in the kitchen or dining room for breakfast. Going into a room such as the living room at a moment so informal as breakfast time was to almost violate its sanctity. During the day, as dad went to work — generally to "the office" — and the kids went off to school, mom might use the living room briefly to watch a favorite soap opera, and she would typically dust and vacuum the living room at least

83

once a week — whether it need-ed it or not. Because of many advances in technology, the vac-uum cleaners of the fifties were far quieter and more efficient than their prewar predecessors. This meant that this chore took much less of mom's time, leaving her an opportunity to socialize with her friends.

If one of mom's friends or neighbors stopped by in the morning for a cup of coffee and a chat, they would typically sit in the kitchen or dining room, for the living room was generally seen as too formal for morning activities. However, in the afternoon, the living room might become the set-ting for a meeting of one of mom's clubs or groups of friends. While mom and her friends

ABOVE: A HOUSEWIFE IN HER MODERN LIVING ROOM WITH HER   *GENERAL ELECTRIC SWIVEL-TOP.*

may have dressed informally for morning coffee and/or housework, an afternoon meeting or "coffee clatch" almost invariably required semiformal attire. For most of the fifties, this meant a dress and dress shoes. Depending on the occasion and the part of the country (the Northeast and the Old South were always more formal than the Midwest and California), it might also mean hat and gloves.

While mom entertained her friends during the day, the kids were almost never permitted to use the living room to entertain their friends. This took place in the kids' bedrooms or the back yard (weather permitting), although the kitchen and dining area were usually open to use by the kids and their friends.

The kids would often be permitted to watch television or do their homework in the living room during the afternoon, but this permission

would usually not be extended if they had friends over to the house.

When he got home from work, dad might sit in his favorite chair in the living room while mom finished making dinner. After dinner, the entire family would retire to the living room to watch television or engage in some other family activity. Because of the growing importance of television to American life in the fifties, many people actually ate dinner in the living room so that they could watch television while eating. This led to the creation of a device called a "TV

85

❋

TOP: A SLEEK SEARS SECTIONAL IN A MODERN LIVING ROOM. OPPOSITE TOP: THE 1956 LEWYT VACUUM WAS CALLED "THE WORLD'S EASIEST-TO-USE CLEANER."

tray," a lightweight aluminum folding tray about 30 inches high that was large enough to accommodate a dinner plate and a side dish, but one had to be careful if a drink was placed on the tray because the lightweight legs were a bit wobbly. Later in the fifties, wooden TV trays would make their appearance, but the vast majority were the lightweight metal ones.

As the average size of houses increased, a separate "TV room" might be set aside for watching television, in which case the living room would remain empty. This was the begin-ning of the evolution of the "family room" concept of the seventies and eighties, during which the living room would evolve into a sort of rarely used museum of family artifacts.

Formal entertaining during the fifties took place in the living room in the evenings and on Sunday afternoons. Women wore dresses and high heels, and men usually wore coats and ties. If the guests being entertained were close friends and in the same age group as mom and dad, then dad might be able to get by with just a sweater, although he would typically wear dress slacks. The kids were often not required to be present unless the guests being entertained were relatives. If they were present, the kids would dress as miniatures of their parents, although boys were not usually required to wear a coat and tie.

Entertaining would often involve the serving of dessert or

ABOVE: THE FIFTIES LIVING ROOM COULD BE COMPLEX AND "BUSY," BUT THE LINES WERE ALL TYPICALLY STRAIGHT AND ANGULAR.

hors d'ouvres. More often than not, coffee would be offered, except on especially warm summer days, when a cold drink would be suggested. The cold drink might be lemonade or a bottled soft drink, but if it was the latter,

it would be served in a glass with ice rather than straight out of the bottle. Ice (or "iced") tea was a favorite in the South, but rarely served elsewhere during the fifties. In the evenings, but almost never on Sundays, alcoholic drinks would be served. Among adults under 30, beer was popular, but wine was rarely served because during the fifties it was hard to get. Imported wine was still expensive and the aggressive mass marketing of California wine did not begin until the seventies.

For adults older than their late twenties, cocktails were the standard fare at evening social events, and decorative decanters containing pop-

ular liquors such as whisky, gin and vodka were often seen displayed on side tables. While the cocktail was not popular with the people who came of age during the sixties and seventies, it enjoyed a renaissance with the young people of the eighties and nineties.

A major difference between the entertaining of the fifties and entertaining at the turn of the century involves smoking. Today, guests assume that smoking is not permitted in a home unless ashtrays are visible, but in the fifties, a host or hostess would be considered remiss for not making sure that there was an adequate number of

87

TOP: THE MODERN GLIDDEN SPRED SATIN PASTELS OF THE LATE FIFTIES COVERED EARLY FIFTIES WALLPAPER. OPPOSITE TOP: A CLASSIC FIFTIES LAMP.

ashtrays for all the guests who needed one.

When the adults of the fifties entertained, it was almost always the wife who served the coffee and the food, although older children were often pressed into service, especially if there were relatives present. The man of the house almost always mixed and served the cocktails, but usually did not get involved in serving the other items unless his wife was overwhelmed by the number of guests. However, in such cases one or two of the women guests would usually offer to help. After all, dad's role in entertaining was that of master of ceremonies. His job was to see that everyone met everyone else. If the people present were associated with his work, he had to make sure that everyone was accorded the proper respect, especially if the boss was present. In such cases, the boss would automatically be the guest of honor. Sunday gatherings often involved the pastor or minister being invited, and at such events, he would be the guest of honor

88

RIGHT AND TOP: CLASSIC FIFTIES STYLING IN SIMMONS FURNITURE THAT INCLUDED LIGHT WOOD END TABLES AND THE FAMOUS SIMMONS HIDE-A-BEDS.

and the host would be charged with the task of assuring that he knew it.

The living room was the place where family life centered in the fifties, an era when families gathered as a group to have a family life. In the fifties, even teenagers spent time with the rest of the family at home. But it was a lifestyle that was fast fading. The intra-family animosity of the late sixties and the disconnectedness of the seventies would create a generation for whom the notion of an intact family functioning together was just an abstract concept. As trite as it may sound, the living room of the fifties marked the golden age of family togetherness. ❊ ❊

89

TOP: ENTERTAINING IN THIS CLASSIC FIFTIES LIVING ROOM, WITH GUESTS AND SERVER DRESSED AS WAS EXPECTED FOR A TYPICAL FIFTIES SOCIAL EVENT.

Watching Television

Television transformed the life and popular culture in a way that no other communications medium ever had, or ever would. During the thirties and forties, radio had been an important part of life for the parents of the baby boomers, but it never had the all-encompassing impact on life that television was to have during the fifties and early sixties. Media critic Marshall McLuhan would suggest in the sixties that the medium *was* the message. In the homes of the fifties, television was certainly *both* the medium and the message.

The first experimental television broadcasts had taken place in the twenties and thirties, but serious commercial television stations did not go on the air until after World War II, and it was not until 1951 that the Federal Communications Commission allocated a sufficient number of VHF frequency bands to make commercial television practical in the United States. Thus it was

90

RIGHT: ENJOYING AN ADMIRAL
BLACK AND WHITE

OPPOSITE: THE STYLISH MOTOROLA
17F4 FOR 1950.

that the new medium was "born" with the fifties.

The number of homes with television sets went from a few hundred, mainly in the New York City area, in 1948 to 3.8 million in 1950, and mushroomed to 32 million in 1955. In 1948, there were fewer than a dozen television stations. By 1950, there were 98, and in 1955, 411 were on the air. The percentage increase during the first five years of the fifties was greater than the percentage increase in the number of stations from 1955 to the end of the century. Meanwhile, the number of television sets in American homes increased tenfold between 1950 and 1955, but between 1955 and the end of the century, there was merely a threefold increase. In 1955 alone, 7.8 million television sets were sold in the United States. Most of these were sold into homes that did not previously have television, meaning that more homes got television for the first time in 1955 alone than in the entire decade from 1985 to 1995.

Early in the fifties, the three major networks that would dominate television until the nineties appeared

LEFT: THE 1951 MAGNAVOX PLAYHOUSE.

and staked out their claim on the airwaves. By mid decade, each of the three would have an affiliate in every major market throughout the country, competing in most cases with just one or two local independents. As the fifties began, the Columbia Broadcasting System (CBS) and the National Broadcasting Company (NBC), both of whom were powerful entities in radio broadcasting were joined by the American Broadcasting Company (ABC) to form a competitive triumvirate that dominated television for the next four decades, until new networks, such as Fox and a myriad of cable channels, changed the comfortable old model forever.

93

Top: In 1952, people gathered in front of the Motorola store to stare in wonder. Opposite Top: Children were especially mesmerized.

While color television existed in the fifties, it was a rarity. Television was, for all intents and purposes, a black and white medium until the mid-sixties. Some programs were filmed in color by far-sighted producers who had the vision to predict both the total replacement of black and white television and the lucrative after-market for reruns. However, most fifties television programming was filmed in black and white, and a great deal of it was live. Often, these live broadcasts were not filmed and were lost forever.

While in hindsight we know that color broadcasting was the first major leap forward in television technology to be demanded and embraced by the public, many other technologies were discussed and studied. In fact, as early as

ABOVE: GATHERED FOR AN AFTER DINNER SNACK, THE WHOLE FAMILY ENJOYED JIMMY DURANTE ON THEIR MOTOROLA 17K7 IN ITS MAHOGANY CASE.

1951, when Zenith introduced its "Black Magic Television" with the "amazing" Blaxide Tube, it included remote control and a "Phonevision" connection. Zenith developed this cable television-type technology and anticipated television on phone lines as early as 1951. Sets with Phonevision connections may still exist in dusty attics, a relic of an innovation that was nearly a half century ahead of its time. Meanwhile, the early, hard-wired remote control led to wireless remote control that was perfected in the eighties and nineties.

In the beginning of the fifties, television programming borrowed heavily from radio, with popular radio entertainers and news anchors making the transition to the new medium. Entertainment in the early fifties was predominantly live, New York-based variety shows that had at least one foot deeply rooted in prewar vaudeville. *Ted Mack's Original Amateur Hour* had its debut in 1948, and *Arthur Godfrey's Talent Scouts*, a virtual clone, went on the air at CBS in 1950. The difference was that Godfrey did not depend solely on fresh talent, but rather kept an ensemble of proven radio stars on hand for frequent repeat appearances. These included singers Connie Francis, Rosemary Clooney and Tony Bennett, as well as Steve Lawrence. Sid Ceasar's *Your Show of Shows* first appeared the same year, also with an ensemble cast that included New York's favorite professional celebrity, Imo-

95

gene Coca, as well as a young comic named Carl Reiner. The writers for Ceasar's show included Woody Allen and Mel Brooks. One of the most important singers of the decade, Perry Como, had his own network show, which also went on the air with CBS in 1950.

Two important former vaudevillians who went on television in 1951 were Red Skelton and Milton Berle. Berle, a professional ham who went by the nickname "Mr. Television," was the host of the Texaco Star Theatre, a show with dancers dressed as filling station attendants singing "We're the men from Texaco, we work from Maine to Mexico."

That legendary entertainer of the early fifties, Jack Benny, also made his network debut in 1951, but the most important and longest-lived of the fifties variety shows was Ed Sullivan's *Toast of the Town*, which dated from 1948, but which became *The Ed Sullivan Show* in 1954. Ed Sullivan had the only variety show of

96

RIGHT: IN 1952, AMERICANS EQUATED THE COSMOS WITH THE FUTURE.

Now...see

Sparton

cosmic eye

television

Thrill to great new 1952 Sparton Cosmic Eye Television. So beautiful in performance, so superbly engineered, with such clear, sharp, flawless pictures *it's like having an eye in the sky.* For a new idea of television engineering refinement, see Sparton Cosmic Eye Television today!

Look for the Cosmic Eye medallion tag identifying these spectacular new models at your Sparton dealer's today. A sign of television perfection!

THE SUPERB

Sparton

SHOW PIECE

OF YOUR HOME

The Lochmoor
21" Mahogany Console

the early crop to survive the fifties. In fact, he would be on the air until 1971.

Elvis Presley, the essential icon of American pop music during the fifties (although he was shunned by almost everyone over 25) came to national popularity mainly through television. Born in Mississippi and raised in Memphis, Tennessee, Elvis was a product of the South in an era when regional cultural phenomena rarely attained national notice. Because the national media was located in New York City, one needed to be accepted and presented by New York in order to be visible nationally. In March 1955, Elvis went north to try out for *Arthur Godfrey's Talent Scouts*, but was given a thumbs down. A year later, Elvis was signed as a guest on *Stage Show*, the variety show hosted by big band greats Tommy Dorsey and Jimmy Dorsey, which originated from CBS Studio 50. Elvis' most famous television appearances were those on *The Ed Sullivan*

97

LEFT: ENJOYING THE 1951 GENERAL ELECTRIC BLACK-DAYLITE TELEVISION.

Show, where his performances are remembered for Sullivan's insistence that the camera not show Elvis' hips, which he shook when he performed. Indeed, Sullivan reportedly did not like "Elvis the Pelvis," nor want him on the show at all. He acquiesced to Elvis' appearance only because of the high ratings of his earlier appearances. After the two men had met, however, Sullivan described Elvis as a "decent, fine boy." Elvis'

final *Ed Sullivan Show* took place on January 6, 1957, cementing his place in the national consciousness and in the folklore of the fifties.

Another long-running fifties variety show, and one that still survives (albeit in a vastly different format), was *The Tonight Show*. It went on the air at NBC in New York in 1954 with Steve Allen as its original host. He would pass the baton to Jack Paar in 1956, who in turn passed it to Johnny Carson in 1962.

Television began playing a pivotal role in the American electoral process during the 1952 presidential campaign, when Dwight Eisenhower, the Republican nominee for president, and his opponent, Gover-

LEFT: DAD ENJOYED THE PAPER AND MOM KNITTED AS THE WHOLE FAMILY ENJOYED THE 1954 CAPEHART CONSOLE SET.

Television waves travel better

on the world's tiniest ball bearings . . .

Electric currents zigzag up to 216 million times a second through the radio frequency coil of the typical FM radio or television circuit. The quality of reception of any set is largely determined by this coil.

The heart of the best radio frequency coil is a small cylinder . . . of insulated, compressed carbonyl iron powder.

Carbonyl iron powder is 98.0% chemically pure iron, in almost perfect spheres—feels finer than a woman's face powder. This form of iron retains its inductive and magnetic properties indefinitely, is stable to temperature extremes, does not deteriorate with use.

Carbonyl iron powder is formed and purified under carefully controlled heats and pressures . . . a difficult and complex process . . . and in this country is made by General Aniline . . . supply source to manufacturers of electronic equipment and television sets.

Today carbonyl iron powder is finding new uses for pharmaceuticals, iron tonics, and the enrichment of bread and other food products.

And carbonyl iron powder is only one of approximately four thousand products of General Aniline . . . whose laboratories make a major contribution to public welfare.

GENERAL ANILINE plants at Rensselaer, N.Y. and Grasselli, N. J. lead the US production of high quality dyestuffs (sold through General Dyestuff Corporation, NYC) . . . the Ansco division at Binghamton, N.Y. is the oldest maker of photographic equipment, cameras, and films . . . the Ozalid division at Johnson City, N.Y. makes facsimile reproducing machines and sensitized papers...Antara Products in New York City develops new product applications.

In a big industry essential to our national economy, General Aniline is a good company to work for and with, buy from and sell to . . . worth knowing and watching!

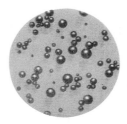

Under a microscope magnifying 750 times, the carbonyl iron powder shows spherical shape.

Electronic wave trap (below) has carbonyl iron powder core.

GENERAL ANILINE & FILM CORPORATION

...From Research to Reality...

230 Park Avenue, New York 17, N. Y.

nor Adlai Stevenson, the Democratic nominee, both used paid television commercials to reach the voters. Television news and public affairs programming was then in its infancy, but the paid television ads drew a great deal of attention.

Both the Democratic and Republican conventions were broadcast in 1952, marking the first time that the American public had seen with their own eyes the process by which candidates were selected. By the late fifties, television was seen as being at least as important as newspapers, and much more important than traditional door-to-door campaigning, as the medium for reaching voters. As the late Theodore H. White, who wrote his famous *Making of the President* books about many key postwar presidential campaigns, said, "Television is the political process; it's the playing field of politics. Today, the action is in the studios, not in the back rooms."

The news was originally covered in 15-minute nightly clips emanating from the three network headquarters in New York. CBS originally used radio

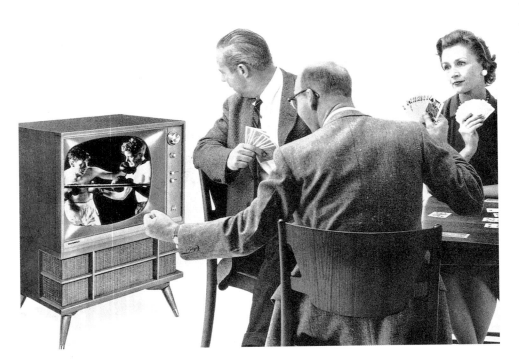

ABOVE: THE MOTOROLA 21CB, WITH ITS THREE BIG SPEAKERS AND "GRAND SLAM PICTURE," WAS HARD TO IGNORE, EVEN DURING A CARD GAME.

legend Edward R. Murrow to anchor the program *See It Now*, which was really a sort of celebration of television and the medium's ability to bring pictures into the homes of regular people. The actual anchor of the 15-minute CBS nightly news for most of the fifties was Douglas Edwards. The well-loved and respected Walter Cronkite did not take over until 1962.

NBC began a 15-minute nightly news program of its own in 1950 with John Cameron Swayze, and in 1956 introduced the best-remembered anchors of the era: Chet Huntley and David Brinkley. Meanwhile, NBC began airing *The Today Show* in 1952, with Dave Garroway and Frank Blair.

The variety shows that dominated the early days of fifties television were soon superceded by that which still continues to be a prime-time staple: the half-hour situation comedy. Best remembered from the fifties are *The Honeymooners* with Jackie Gleason and, of course, *I Love Lucy*, which went on the air in 1951 with Lucille Ball and Desi Arnaz.

These programs had their roots in the variety shows insofar as they were set in New York and seemed to take it for granted that New York was both familiar to and *important* to the viewing audience. However, as television stations sprung up across the country, a new national cul-

101

ture emerged, and as a barometer of this, a new genre of television situation programs emerged.

The television genre that most characterized the fifties were the half-hour family situation programs. They were funny, but they were not considered comedies because they didn't rely on gags as *I Love Lucy* did. They were occasionally seriously dramatic, but they were not serious dramas. The family situation shows showed "typical" American families living typical fifties lives in typical American suburbs that could have been anywhere in the country. They were designed not to show us a stylized family in New York City, but an average family that could very well be living in a neighborhood just across the town where we lived. Among the best of this genre were *Father Knows Best, Leave*

it to Beaver, Ozzie and Harriet and *The Donna Reed Show.*

Father Knows Best went on the air in 1954, with Robert Young, Jane Wyatt, Elinor Donahue, Billy Gray and Lauren Chapin portraying the Anderson family. The Andersons lived in Springfield, which could have been in any state because most states have a Springfield that was a comfortably prosperous middle class town during the fifties. Of course, during the eighties and nineties, Springfield was home to television's dysfunctional Simpson family, which was designed as a deliberate parody of families such as the Andersons.

Leave it to Beaver starred Hugh Beaumont, Barbara Billingsley, Jerry Mathers and Tony Dow as the Cleaver family. (Mathers was "the Beaver," the youngest of the two "typical" brothers.) The Cleavers' home was in Mayfield, which, like the Andersons' Springfield, was a town that could have been anywhere, for there were families like the Cleavers everywhere during the fifties.

The Donna Reed Show, which appeared in 1958, rather late in the decade, starred Donna Reed, as well as Carl Betz, Shelley Fabares, Paul Peterson and Patti Peterson as the imaginary and

103

TOP: THE ZENITH BLACK MAGIC TELEVISION OF 1951 WAS VERY STYLISH. OPPOSITE: MOTOROLA'S 17F5 CONSOLE OF 1950 ALSO HAD A PHONOGRAPH.

a pop singer, part of an early wave of Elvis imitators, and he also played himself doing that on television.

In all of their family situation shows, the families represented an ideal of what American families were supposed to be and, for the most part, actually were. The dads all went to work at white collar jobs, and mom stayed home to do housework in a dress and high heels. The kids went to school and came home to freshly baked cookies. Dad almost never stayed late at the office, and family meals — both breakfast and dinner — were the norm. Family problems were almost never major crises, and they were always resolved happily in 24 minutes.

If the family situation programs were a stylized view of real life in the fifties, the most prominent television fantasy was the Western. Why this was is uncertain. There were memorable police dramas, such as *Dragnet* with Jack

truly mythical (in all senses of the word) Stone family. Of this ensemble, Shelley Fabares would blossom during the sixties as a B movie and television starlet who starred opposite Elvis Presley in three of his forgettable formula pictures. The Stones lived in Hilldale, which was a name and a place that were typical of the developed housing tracts that had appeared in the fifties.

Ozzie and Harriet starred Ozzie Nelson, Harriet Nelson, David Nelson and Ricky (later Rick) Nelson essentially as themselves. The show went on the air in 1952, and David and Rick essentially grew up playing themselves growing up on television. Late in the fifties, Rick became

104

❈

Webb, *M Squad* with Lee Marvin and *Perry Mason* with Raymond Burr, but for some reason, the Western was the most important dramatic genre on television during the fifties. Perhaps this was because the fifties were a decade of deliberate American cultural self-obsession, and the Westerns were completely and utterly an American genre.

There were three eras of television Western. First was the "Hero" Western, next the "Situation" Western, and finally, the "Family" Western, which was almost like a *Father Knows Best* set in the Wild West. The Hero Westerns first appeared in 1949-1953. The most characteristic of these was certainly *The Lone Ranger* with Clayton Moore and Jay Silverheels as the Lone Ranger and his faithful Indian (there were no Native Americans yet) sidekick, Tonto. Among the other important Hero Westerns were *Hopalong Cassidy*, starring William Boyd (who went by the name Hopalong Cassidy); *The Cisco Kid,* with Duncan Renaldo and Leo Carrillo; *Annie Oakley,* with Gail Davis; *Kit Carson,* with Bill Williams and Don Diamond; *Wild Bill Hickock,* with Guy Madison and Andy Devine; and, of course, *Roy Rogers,* with the "King of the Cowboys" himself and his real-life wife, Dale Evans.

Wyatt Earp, which first appeared in 1955, starred Hugh O'Brien in a series that was a transition between the Hero and Situation Western. Of the latter genre, the most important program, if not the most important television Western of all time, was *Gunsmoke*. It originated on the radio in 1952, with William Conrad heading the cast, and went to television in 1955, with James Arness as Dodge City's Marshal Matt Dillon.

Other members of the cast were Dennis Weaver as the Marshal's faithful sidekick, Milburn Stone as Doc Adams and Amanda Blake as Miss Kitty, who owned the Long Branch Saloon. The "situation" on *Gunsmoke* was simply that Marshal Dillon was protecting Dodge City from bad guys, who always failed within the duration of the show to do their evil to the somewhat genteel television version of what had actually been a very rough cowtown. In *Have Gun Will Travel*, Richard Boone portrayed a mysterious hired gun named Paladin, who lived as a gentleman in a San Francisco apartment until hired to right a wrong. He then dressed in his all-black cowboy gear and rode east to the Wild West.

Wanted Dead or Alive was an early career vehicle for Steve McQueen, who

106

LEFT: THE 1951 MAGNAVOX PLAYHOUSE.

played a bounty hunter. *Wagon Train*, with Ward Bond and Robert Horton, had life on a wagon train as its in-motion situation, and *Rawhide*, with Eric Fleming and a young Clint Eastwood, was set on an endless cattle drive. All of these were stylized portrayals of realistic situations that actually did occur in the West of the nine-teenth century. Among the first of the Westerns with a family situation was *The Rifleman*, which appeared in 1958 with Chuck Connors as Lucas McCain and Johnny Crawford as his son, Mark McCain. The most important Western television family, though, was the Cartwrights. While *Bonanza* first appeared in 1959, Lorne Greene as

107

TOP: A COWGIRL AND A GENERAL ELECTRIC BLACK-DAYLITE TEAM UP TO ENTERTAIN. OPPOSITE TOP: WATCHING HOPALONG CASSIDY ON A 1950 ARVIN SET.

Ben Cartwright, Pernell Roberts as Adam, Dan Blocker as "Hoss" and Michael Landon as "Little Joe" had their greatest impact during the sixties, when *Bonanza* was the highest rated show for several seasons. Curiously, there was no "mother" figure on either *The Rifleman* or *Bonanza*.

The fifties are recalled as the golden age of the television, and indeed, the impact of television on American life during the fifties was profound. Television arrived on the scene and was installed in more homes and at a faster rate than any other communications medium ever. It had taken decades for telephones to become as common as television sets did in the first few years of the fifties. The television revolution of the early fifties can be (and often has been) compared to the personal computer revolution of the eighties or the Internet craze of the nineties, but in neither case did as many homes embrace the new medium as fast as the American families of the fifties embraced television.

Once embraced, television changed American culture by homogenizing it. Families gathered around television sets in New Hampshire watched the same programs — and the same commercials — on the same day as families in Texas, Oregon or Minnesota. Television helped to create a national culture, and the Americans of the fifties were the first to experience such a phenomenon. The baby boomers who grew up during the fifties had never known any different, and this would serve to shape the future. ❊ ❊

TOP: BY 1958, RCA WAS PRODUCING COLOR SETS AND NBC WAS BROADCASTING ITS NBC MATINEE THEATER WITH "MORE THAN 150 PLAYS IN COLOR."

Nobody touches her new Admiral TV...

(it's wireless remote controlled)

The Rutherford, High Fidelity TV with Son-R.

New 1959 Admiral TV

High Fidelity Picture! High Fidelity Sound! Son-R Remote Control *AT NO EXTRA COST*

Announcing the first really new kind of television in 7 years! Brilliantly alive high fidelity pictures and 4-speaker high fidelity sound. And you never have to touch the set. It's remote controlled with the *wireless* Son-R in your hand.

Son-R adjusts volume to not just one level like ordinary remote controls—but to 4 levels! One push button gives you all 4... *silence, whisper-soft, normal talking range, and full room volume.* Ultrasonic magic works silently to turn TV on-off and change channels in either direction. Operates from anywhere in the room. Stations always come in sharply fine tuned!

All this at no extra cost. It's standard equipment on new 1959 Admiral High Fidelity TV. Wide selection of Slimline, fine furniture models with the jeweler's touch. Also decorator-approved Originals. See, hear this new kind of quality TV today.

Push button...click...there's your channel! Tune perfectly from your arm chair with Son-R remote control. Tiny as milady's compact. No wires! No batteries! No tubes to wear out! Automatic 4-level sound control, originated by Admiral. When not in use, Son-R slips into *magnetic* pocket on side of set.

wireless! world's smallest!

The Wilshire (CHS21H77) with Son-R. Slimmer than ever cabinet. Mahogany and cherry finished veneers. 4 hi-fi speakers. Extra hi-fi amplifier. 20,000 volt picture power. Touch-a-matic bar tuning. Stereophonic phono jack. New 110° picture tube. 21 in. overall diagonal, 262 sq. in. viewable area.

MARK OF QUALITY THROUGHOUT THE WORLD **Admiral**®

SOLD IN 90 COUNTRIES...MANUFACTURED IN U.S.A., AUSTRALIA, ARGENTINA, BRAZIL, CANADA, ITALY, MEXICO, PHILIPPINES, AND URUGUAY.

109

The Bed and Bath

The first thing that should be said about bedrooms of the fifties is that they were for sleeping. Indeed, most people have always spent more time in their bedrooms sleeping than engaged in any other activities. It was just that the culture of the fifties went out of its way to project an image of bedrooms being free of any implied sexuality. In fact, the general portrayal of bedrooms during the fifties seemed to be very *explicit* in its projection of an

absence of sexuality. The married couples on the favorite television shows slept in separate beds, and so did married couples portrayed in most media. A great many real married couples slept in separate beds too, but somehow, the television couples seemed to have acquired kids somewhere, and the real married couples parented the vast baby boom. These baby boom children of the parents in separate beds would launch the sexual revolution of the sixties

110

❈

RIGHT: A MODERN FIFTIES BEDROOM IN SOOTHING BLUE.

OPPOSITE: A BEDROOM WITH A RAYBELLE LINOLEUM FLOOR BY ARMSTRONG, 1955.

and seventies, and they would be sure that they were right. By the end of the century, with the baby boom generation in middle age, there was once again an emphasis on the importance of

that "good night's sleep" that their mothers had told them about. Bedrooms were for sleeping.

Whether the beds in the fifties bedrooms were twins or kings, they were usually the least "Bauhaus" of the furniture of the fifties. To a greater degree than in the other rooms in the fifties home, they retained the little design embellishments that seemed to be from an earlier time. There were lathe-turned posts on the beds, especially the kids' beds, and there were con-toured headboards. Occasionally, heavy drapery survived from the forties, and canopy beds were fair-ly common. Mom probably remembered wanting one when she was growing up in the thirties or forties, and now, by golly, she was going to have one. If mom had wanted one as a girl, or even if she hadn't, she

LEFT: SEPARATE BEDS WERE TYPICAL.

would be certain to make one available for her daughter. Boys, if there were two in the family, tended to like bunk beds.

It was usually mom who decorated the fifties master bedroom, and the colors that mom specified were those that were typical of the era, such as turquoise blue, mint green or pink. Dad probably grumbled about pink, but in many cases, mom got her way on matters of the home. Wallpaper was a holdover from the earlier times that survived through the fifties, but floral patterns reminiscent of the forties gave way to simple stripes and bold patterns. The abstract florals and vibrant primary colors were to be sixties phenomena.

The furniture that rounded out the bedroom set usually included a dresser and a pair of end tables, as well as a pair of matching modern lamps and possibly a dressing table for mom. The kids' rooms were usually, in the vernacular of the nineties, very gender specific. Sis would have a room that was very pink, with ruffles and bows, while her brother's room was painted in more earthy colors and decorated with curtains and bedspread that expressed a Wild West or outer space theme. Popular television programs, especially Westerns, tended to have licensed merchandise, so a Wyatt Earp bedspread was possible. Of

113

TOP: MATCHING PINK WALLPAPER AND BED, POPULAR WITH FIFTIES TEENAGERS. OPPOSITE TOP: WAKING UP TO A SONG WITH A TELECHRON CLOCK RADIO.

course, the "Davy Crockett" look was very popular with boys in the mid-fifties. Down the hall in the bathroom, the color schemes were similar to those of the bedrooms. Unlike kitchen appliances, which still remained in their familiar, albeit antiseptic white for much of the decade, bathroom fixtures were already becoming colored in the forties. Hues such as turquoise blue, mint green or pink appeared, and yellow — American-Standard called theirs "Manchu" yellow — was popular. As with kitchen appliances, however, avocado green was popular in living room upholstery and towels, but it would not appear until the late sixties in bathroom fixtures. The phrase "full color bathroom" was coined by Universal-Rundle of New Castle, Pennsylvania, who claimed to be the first to offer color fixtures. In 1952, the company announced Azure Blue, Verdant Green and Desert Tan as well as white.

ABOVE: IN 1952, UNIVERSAL-RUNDLE OFFERED A VARIETY OF COLORS IN FIXTURES, BUT EVEN WITH WHITE, THE RIGHT ACCENTS MADE A BATHROOM BRIGHT.

The sales of bathroom fixtures did not approach that of kitchen appliances. The reason was simple. Whereas new homes required new appliances as well as new bathroom fixtures, people who remodeled older homes upgraded their kitchens because of greatly improved appliance technology. With bathrooms, basic technology remained the same.

There was a revolution in bathtub shapes as new bathtub styles were introduced. These included American-Standard's Neo-Angle bathtub, which was essentially a four-foot square in which a person reclined diagonally. It fit neatly in a corner, allowing more useful floor space in the room. Eljer Plumbing Fixtures of Ford City, Pennsylvania addressed the growing needs of baby boom parents with their Legation bathtub,

which had an integral end seat and rim seat, which were "ideal for bathing children."

The children whose early memories are of bathing in vividly-colored tubs and falling asleep under Davy Crockett bedspreads grew up as part of a generation that experienced a level of prosperity about which their parents could only dream. That which was the dream come true for the baby boom parents is that which forms the fond memories of the baby boomers. ✳ ✳

115

✳

Back Yard Fun

A major reason for the dramatic shift of urban population from the cities to the suburbs in the fifties had to do with the notion of having some open space around the house in the form of a yard. While the familiar housing developments of the eighties and nineties often a have smaller usable yard space than do the older row houses in the cities, the new housing tracts built in the fifties had substantial yard space. In addition, many homes had a poured concrete pad

called a patio, which was useful for placing a picnic table or outdoor chairs.

At the beginning of the fifties, most lawn furniture was made of wood or steel. The wood provided a "rustic" look, but the steel just rusted. Advances in materials technology which occurred as a result of World War II made possible a new generation of lawn furniture. While aluminum would corrode over time, it did so much more slowly than iron rusted, and it did not leave ugly

116

✳

RIGHT: BRINGING TELEVISION TO A BARBEQUE.

OPPOSITE: POOLTIME FUN WITH MOM.

brown marks on the patio. Plastics, especially vinyl, were becoming more and more durable and, during the fifties, they were being adapted for many uses around the home and in the yard. Plastic lawn and patio furniture was inexpensive, and best of all, it was available in the brilliant colors that people of the fifties wanted. In turn, American Cyanamid developed its trademark UV-Absorbers to prevent ultraviolet radiation from the sun from discoloring plastics. In the warmer months during the fifties, families would gather outside on the patio or on the lawn. Plastic wading pools would be a standard fixture in back yards across the land as the baby boom toddlers went outside to splash and frolic. The back yard was also an ideal place for the kids' birthday parties. For those baby boomers who were lucky enough to have been born between May and September, blowing out candles at a back yard picnic table is part of the fabric of their memories of the fifties.

LEFT: BATHTIME FOR BOWSER.

Cooking and eating outdoors was a major cultural trend that spread widely during the fifties. The back yard barbecue became part of the American lifestyle. At first, there were a lot of jokes about families who had gone to the expense to install very modern kitchens in their homes, yet they cooked and ate outdoors under comparatively primitive conditions. Obviously, outdoor barbecues on sunny days were fun and something that people did to make use of the outdoor space for which they had chosen the suburbs. Whereas the kitchen was mom's domain, and she was almost always in charge of cooking the meals indoors, it was dad who typically donned an apron and chef's hat outdoors. The social critics waxed on about his primal need to be involved

119

TOP: *MAKING FRIENDS ACROSS THE FENCE.* OPPOSITE TOP: *HE LOOKED SHARP, BUT SOMETIMES DAD WASN'T PAYING ATTENTION TO HIS GRILL.*

with open fire, but dad had fun firing up the coals and scorching the steaks or burgers for the family or friends. While the back yard barbecue was the most informal social gathering for the typical American suburban family during the fifties, dad would usually wear slacks and a sport shirt rather than jeans and a t-shirt as one would expect today. Even at an informal occasion such as a barbecue, there was a sense of style about the fifties that has been lost in subsequent decades.

Dad also took the lead in chores associated with the yard. First and foremost there was lawn care. This appealed to dad's inherent longing for tools and machinery. The gasoline powered lawn mower proliferated across the suburban landscape during the fifties, and machines such as roto-tillers and garden tractors were available as well. In the fall, leaf raking was dad's number one outdoor chore, and in the winter, he shoveled snow from the sidewalk and driveway. If he didn't the kids often did. Such tasks were all a part of the new suburban lifestyle. ❄ ❄

120

LEFT: FUN WITH THE 1954 SIMPLICITY LAWN TRACTOR.

ABOVE: THE PATIO WAS THE CENTER OF FAMILY ACTIVITIES ON WARM AFTERNOONS. OPPOSITE TOP: DAD AT WORK WITH HIS 1956 LAWN BOY MOWER.

Family Car Trips

As automobile ownership increased during the fifties, Americans became more mobile, and the family car trip became an important facet of family life. Like television watching, car trips became an aspect of family life that had not existed before on the scale that it would during and beyond the fifties

The cars of the fifties were bigger, more powerful and more fun to travel in than their predecessors. As we shall discover in this chapter, the roads themselves would improve dramatically during the fifties as Americans hit the road.

Also along the way, a new type of infrastructure would be introduced to cater to the new

122

❋

ON THE ROAD, FROM THE HEARTLAND OF INDIANA (RIGHT) TO THE CASCADES (OPPOSITE).

United States by 1959. Restaurants offering quick meals would proliferate. Diners and hamburger stands would evolve from hoky mom-and-pop places to slick, assembly line operations. Individual fast food restaurants would soon be replaced by chains. One of the first was Dairy Queen, which had 1,156 franchises in 1950 and over 3,000 by 1959. That favorite of American fast food chains, McDonald's, was founded by Dick and Mac McDonald in 1948 in San Bernardino, California, and licensed as a chain by Ray Kroc in 1954. By 1959, Kroc had more than 100 restaurants.

motoring Americans. When it came to buying gasoline, service stations — with the emphasis on *service* — would replace the old fashioned filling stations almost entirely. Motels, largely unknown in 1950, would outnumber hotels in most of the

The story of American families on the road in the fifties is very much part of going home to the fifties. For Americans, newly mobile at

124

LEFT: OFF ON THE HONEYMOON, 1957.

the dawn of the fifties, the "going" was as essential to going home as was "home." In this section, we are indebted to *Special Resource Study Route 66,* published by the United States Department of the Interior, National Park Service

Mobility was a child of prosperity because Americans could now afford cars in bigger numbers, but a big part of mobility was the highways on which to drive the cars. During World War II, regular highway programs had ceased because highway materials and personnel were used to build access roads for war production and military needs. With rationing of gasoline and tires, and no new automobiles being manufactured, the use of mass transit in urban areas and long distance buses in rural areas increased. Between 1941 and 1946, transit ridership grew by 65 percent, to an all-time high of 23.4 billion trips annually. When the war came to an end, the pent-up demand for homes and automobiles ushered in the suburban boom era. Automobile production jumped from a mere 70,000 in 1945 to 2.1 million in 1946, and 3.5 million in 1947. Highway travel reached its prewar peak by 1946 and began to climb at six percent per year. This rate would continue through the fifties and

TOP: VACATIONING WITH GRAMPA. OPPOSITE TOP: SAUZER'S WAFFLE SHOP ON ROUTE 30 IN SCHERERVILLE, INDIANA SERVED "HOME-STYLE" FOOD.

sixties and not falter until the energy crisis of 1973-1974, when temporary gas shortages and the misguided two decade adoption of the ridiculous 55 mph national speed limit altered a way of life and made long distance family car trips difficult and impractical. It was not until 1996 that Americans would again enjoy the freedom to use the roads that they'd enjoyed in the fifties and sixties.

When postwar prosperity put more Americans in cars than ever before, people put their cars on the road and discovered a highway system built for the traffic levels of the twenties and early thirties — and which had deteriorated to boot. In the late forties, the nation's highways were in poor shape to handle the increasing load of traffic. Little had been done during the war to improve the highways and wartime traffic had exacerbated their condition. Moreover, the growth of development in the suburbs occurred in formerly rural areas where highways did not have the capacity to carry the resulting traffic. Suburban traffic quickly overwhelmed the existing two-lane country roads.

Transit facilities, too, experienced significant wear and tear during the war from extended use and deferred maintenance. This resulted in deteriora-

126

LEFT: *A CLOGGED TWO-LANE, 1950.*

tion in transit's physical plant by war's end. Pent-up wage demands of transit employees were met, causing nearly a 50 percent increase in average fares by 1950. This further contributed to a decline in ridership.

The postwar era concentrated on dealing with the problems resulting from suburban growth and resulting from the return to a peacetime economy. Many of the planning activities which had to be deferred during the war resumed with renewed vigor and included the milestone Interregional Highways Report. The Federal Aid Highway Act of 1944 was passed in anticipation of the transition to a postwar economy and to prepare for the expected growth in traffic. The act significantly increased the funds authorized for federal-aid highway programs from $137,500 in 1942 and 1943, and no funds in 1944 and 1945, to $500,000 annually for 1946 through 1948. The act also recognized the growing complexity of the highway program. Federal aid was authorized for primary roads and also for a secondary system of farm-to-market and feeder roads. For the first time, federal aid funds up to one-third the cost could be used to acquire rights-of-way for new highways.

Conceptually, the most important innovation that was to be adopted by highway planners

127

and authorized by Congress in the Federal Aid Highway Act of 1944 was a national system of Interstate Highways. This system, which we now take for granted, was to be a revolutionary change in American culture. Like the ubiquity of television, the revolutionary ease of travel made possible by Interstate Highways was first experienced by the American people during the fifties.

The National System of Interstate Highways, "not to exceed 40,000 miles," was in the Federal Aid Highway Act of 1944, but money was not authorized for construction of the system. However, based on the recommendations of the United States Bureau of Public Roads and the Department of Defense, a 37,700-mile system was adopted in 1947. The Department of Defense was now involved, because it could see the value of an efficient highway network in time of war. The actual routing of the Interstate Highway System was chosen by individual states with the approval of the federal Bureau of Public Roads.

Funds were appropriated, but at fairly low levels until the early fifties. To

LEFT: THE FAMILY PICNIC, 1956.

secure a significant increase in funding, a major national lobbying effort was launched in 1952 by the Highway Users Conference under the title "Project Adequate Roads." President Dwight Eisenhower appointed a national advisory committee under General Lucius D. Clay, which, in 1955, produced a report called *A Ten-Year National Highway Program.* This report recommended building a 37,000-mile Interstate Highway System, using bonds to fund the $23 billion cost. However, it was the Federal Aid Highway Act of 1956 that finally changed the funding base and made the Interstate Highways possible. The act was the culmination of two decades of studies and negotiation. It launched the largest public works program yet undertaken.

The construction of the National System of Interstate and Defense Highways was a herculean effort on the order of the Manhattan Project of the forties, or the Apollo Program of the sixties, and infinitely more useful to Americans than either of these.

Mass federal sponsorship for an Interstate system of divided highways markedly increased with President Eisenhower's second term in the White House. As the Supreme Allied Commander in Europe during World War II, then-General Eisenhower had returned from Germany very impressed by the strategic value of the German Autobahn superhighway system, which was probably the best highway system in the world at the

129

improve the defense capabili-
ties of the nation's highways.

With the Federal Aid
Highway Act of 1956, con-
struction of the National System of Interstate and
Defense Highways shifted
into high gear. The act
increased the authorized system extent to 41,000 miles.
This system was planned to
link 90 percent of the cities
with populations of 50,000 or greater
and many smaller cities and towns. The act also
authorized the expenditure of $24.8 billion in 13
fiscal years, from 1957 to 1969, at a 90 percent
federal share. The symbolic completion of the
Interstate Highway system, which was largely
built in the fifties and sixties was intended to
come in 1972, but it would take much longer. The
symbolic end finally came in October 1984 when

time. "During
World War II," he
recalled later, "I saw the superlative system of
German national highways crossing that country
and offering the possibility, often lacking in the
United States, to drive with speed and safety at
the same time."

130

The heightened global tension hastened by
the Cold War affirmed Eisenhower's resolve to

the final section of the original US Highway 66 was replaced by Interstate 40 at Williams, Arizona.

In the fifties, as the two-lane highways yielded to the wider, smooth-surfaced, all-weather Interstate Highways of a highly urbanized, postwar America, one of the older highways emerged as an element of fifties folklore. US Highway 66 had existed since the twenties, but it was not until the late forties and fifties, with the increased mobility of most Americans, and the general east-to-west migration of the fifties, that the folklore of Route 66 became part of American mass culture. Americans had assumed an identity of a people on the move, constantly in hope of job opportunities and new beginnings beyond the western horizon.

The trend westward continued through the fifties, and it included a cultural shift that was perhaps best illustrated by "America's favorite pastime," when the Brooklyn Dodgers moved to Los Angeles in 1958 and the New York Giants moved west to San Francisco in 1958.

Now replaced by Interstate Highways 40, 44 and 55, Route 66 was America's first continuously paved link between Los Angeles and Chicago, the gateway to the industrialized Northeast, and the route was and is the shortest all-weather route between these two cities. To the average motorist the importance of Route 66 was that it reduced cross-country travel between the Midwest and the Pacific Coast by at least two hundred miles. Beginning at the corner of Jackson Boulevard and Michigan Avenue in Chicago,

TOP: THE SATELLITE MOTEL, KNOWN AS "ERICK'S LATEST AND FINEST," OFFERED TELEVISION AND "REFRIGERATED AIR" ON ROUTE 66 IN ERICK, OKLAHOMA.

Route 66 wound 2,400 miles across America to the Pacific Ocean at Santa Monica, California. Its oiled surface etched a trail across the landscape by way of St. Louis, Tulsa, Oklahoma City, Amarillo, Albuquerque and Gallup, New Mexico, as well as Flagstaff, Arizona. From Kingman, Arizona, it ran through Barstow, San Bernardino,

and Pasadena into Los Angeles and to the oceanside at Santa Monica. Its broad, sweeping arc connected Illinois with Missouri, then sliced through the agricultural Midwest, rolled across the Great Plains, and crossed the desert Southwest. To many Americans, Route 66 represented more than just an official highway. According to cultural geographer Arthur Krim, Route 66 was "the symbolic river of America moving west in the auto age of the twentieth century." For others, the well traveled public road was a commercial lifeline. From its inception in 1926, US Highway 66 was designed to connect rural communities to their respective metropolitan capitals. In so doing, gas stations, motels, "mom and pop" restaurants, and grocery stores were built in the hope of servicing an increasingly mobile public.

Route 66 was the result of America's infatuation with rapid

132

LEFT: THE DE ANZA ON ROUTE 66 IN ALBUQUERQUE.

mobility, mass transportation, and technological change. Historian Richard Davies wrote, "The automobile constituted a personalized urban mass transit system, allowing the owner to travel whenever or wherever he desired." Moreover, it provided a personal means of escape from the congestion of metropolitan America. One significant effect of the increased use of the automobile, according to Davies, was to reduce cross-country travel from an adventure of the affluent and stout hearted to a relatively inexpensive and common occurrence.

Officially, the numerical designation 66 was assigned to the Chicago-to-Los Angeles route in the summer of 1926. With that designation came its acknowledgement as one of the nation's principal east-west arteries. However, for the most part, United States 66 was just an assignment of a number to an already existing network of state-managed, two-lane roads, most of which were in poor condition.

The diagonal configuration of Route 66 was particularly significant to the trucking industry, which by 1930 had come to rival the railroads for preeminence in the American shipping industry.

133

TOP: A FAMILY CAR TRIP IN THE 1957 CHEVROLET BEL AIR. OPPOSITE TOP: ROUTE 66 FORMED THE MAIN STREET OF GALLUP, NEW MEXICO.

The abbreviated route between Chicago and the Pacific Coast traversed essentially flat prairie lands and enjoyed a more temperate climate than northern highways, which made it especially appealing to truckers. The Illinois Motor Vehicles

Division reported that between Chicago and St. Louis trucks increased from approximately 1,500 per day in 1931 to 7,500 per day in 1941.

Increased federal commitment began with the Great Depression and the national appeal for emergency federal relief measures. In his famous social commentary, *The Grapes of Wrath*, John Steinbeck proclaimed US Highway 66 "the Mother Road." Steinbeck's classic 1939 novel, combined with the 1940 film recreation of the epic odyssey, served to immortalize Route 66 in the American consciousness. An estimated 210,000 people migrated to California to escape the despair of the Dust Bowl.

America's mobilization for war after Pearl Harbor underscored the necessity for a systematic network of roads and highways. The War Department's expropriation of the nation's railways left a transportation vacuum

LEFT: SERVICE WITH A SMILE AT THE GULF STATION, 1951.

in the West that only the trucking industry could fill. Manufacturers suffered critical shortages of steel, glass, and rubber during the war years, and plants in Detroit converted to the production of tanks, aircraft engines, ordnance, and troop transports.

The social dislocation and uprooting of millions of Americans that began during the Great Depression and continued through World War II did not abate with the surrender of Germany and Japan. After the war Americans were more mobile than ever before. Thousands of soldiers, sailors and airmen who received military training in California, Texas and the Southwest abandoned the harsh winters of Chicago, New York City, and Boston for the "barbecue culture" of the Southwest and the West. Again, for many, Route 66 facilitated their relocation. One such emigrant was Robert William "Bobby" Troup, Jr., of Harrisburg, Pennsylvania. A former pianist with the Tommy Dorsey band, Troup penned the classic song "Route 66," a lyrical road map of the now famous cross-country road in which the words, "Get your kicks on Route 66" became a catch phrase for

135

❉

countless motorists who moved back and forth
between Chicago and the Pacific Coast. One
scholar likened the popular recording released in
1946 by Nat King Cole one week after Troup's

arrival in Los Angeles to "a cartographic ballad."
No doubt Bobby Troup's musical rendition provided a convenient mental road map for those
who followed him west.

It was during the postwar decades that the
population shift from "snowbelt" to "sunbelt"
reached its zenith. Census figures for these years
revealed population growth along Route 66
ranged from 40 percent in New Mexico to 74 percent in Arizona. Because
of the great influx of people during
the war years, California claimed
over half of the total population of
the West in the fifties. It should, of
course be added that Route 66 was
not alone in carrying these people.

Perhaps equally important
(although not celebrated in song)
was US Highway 40 that ran from
Atlantic City, New Jersey to San
Francisco, and which was replaced

136

✳

LEFT: ON THE ROAD WITH AMEX TRAVELERS CHEQUES.

by Interstate 80 in the sixties. There was also Route 10 (later Interstate 90) that linked Boston to Seattle, and Route 30 (now Interstate 84) that departed from Route 40 at Salt Lake City to run toward Portland, Oregon.

Just as New Deal work relief programs provided employment with the construction and the maintenance of Route 66, the appearance of countless tourist courts, garages, and diners promised sustained economic growth after the road's completion. If military use of the highway during wartime ensured the early success of roadside businesses, the demands of the new tourism industry in the postwar decades gave rise to modern facilities that guaranteed long-term prosperity. The evolution of these facilities is well represented in the roadside architecture along US Highways 66 and 40. For example, most Americans who drove the route did not stay in hotels. In the fifties, they preferred motels, which evolved from earlier features of the American roadside, such as the auto camp and the tourist court. Like hotels, the motels offered rooms, but unlike hotels, they offered a place to park a car

137

TOP: THE THRILL OF THE OPEN ROAD WITH THE TOP DOWN. OPPOSITE TOP: THE CHIEF DINER IN DURANGO, COLORADO WAS "KNOWN COAST TO COAST."

Route 66 and many points of interest along the way were familiar landmarks by the time a new generation of postwar motorists hit the road in the fifties. Many drew upon memories from excursions with their parents. World War II transformed the American public from a predominantly agricultural-industrial laboring class to an urban-technological society with increasing leisure and recreational time. In the fifties, the American tourists' fondness for automobile travel

that was near the room. Motels also often had additional amenities, such as adjoining restaurants and souvenir shops, but they also frequently had swimming pools, a family favorite.

ABOVE: ARRIVING AT AN ARIZONA MOTEL ON A CROSS-COUNTRY ROAD TRIP IN THE 1956 PONTIAC STRATO-STREAK WAGON.

and their enjoyment of sightseeing made them ideal targets for the service industries that cropped up along US Highways 66 and 40, and other such roads.

To the average motoring family in the fifties, a trip down the highway — whatever the numerical designation — was an adventure through mainstream America accentuated by quaint, mom-and-pop motels, fast becoming the precursors to the Motel 6s and Econo-Lodges; the quirky all-night diners that would be replaced by chain restaurants; and, of course, the local curio shops that would one day be replaced by souvenir shops that sell wares that are indigenous to the place where they're sold only in the decals on the coffee mugs and t-shirts.

The fifties were a special time, and, as the fifties family car trip clearly demonstrated, America was a special place. Somewhere out on the last vestiges of Route 66, US Highway 40, or even congested US Highway 1, there may be a carefully disguised remnant of a bygone era, where a hard right turn will put you on that road that will take you home to the fifties. To paraphrase that favorite song from the previous decade that was still popular at Christmastime through the fifties, "We'll be going home to the fifties, if only in our dreams." ❉ ❉

139

TOP: INTO THE SUNSET IN A 1957 FORD CUSTOM 300 FORDOR SEDAN. OPPOSITE TOP: THE BEL AIR PALMS MOTEL IN EL MONTE, CALIFORNIA.

The Future

Never had a decade ended amid so much optimism for the following decade than did the fifties. The wave of prosperity that had been experienced on the personal level by the vast majority of Americans inspired an excitement and an anticipation unlike anything that had been known before. It was *Pax Americana*. The United States led the world in everything, and soon the United States would lead the world to the moon and beyond. Those who were adults in 1959 remembered that 1929 ended with the world spiralling into Depression and 1939 with the world spiralling into a global war. Even 1949 was marked by uncertainty. Not so 1959. Everyone fully expected the good news to last indefinitely. In 1960, America would elect a new leader who promised an exciting "New Frontier." The future had never looked better than it did on December 31, 1959, but who could predict that it never would again? Americans did reach the moon, but we withdrew and never went back.

what's all this TALK about Rockets TO THE Moon?

140

❋

LEFT: ADVERTISING ULTRALITE INSULATION, 1950.

Within a few years, crises such as Cuba, Berlin and Vietnam would tear at the fabric of American society and tarnish the golden dream that had come true during the fifties. Assassinations and Watergate would destroy our belief in our own institutions. Perhaps it is in these disappointments that we are best able to appreciate how truly wonderful the fifties had been to Americans, with their two-car garages and their intact families.

Maybe we really were naive back then, but maybe the only thing wrong with that naivete was our belief that those days would live on as more than just the golden memories. ❊ ❊

141

TOP: A DRAMATIZATION OF THE "TIME PROOF" BODY BY FISHER IN THE 1959 PONTIAC STAR CHIEF VISTA.

Index

OVERLEAF: GOOD NIGHT, SWEET DREAMS. DREAM GOOD DREAMS ABOUT THE DECADE WHEN DREAMS CAME TRUE.